The Cosmic Wisdom Bey

Best Wishes

Arthur C. Author

First Published in Great Britain by

SOLOS PRESS

Distributed by Ashgrove Distribution,

4 Brassmill Centre, Brassmill Lane,

Bath, Avon, BA! 3JN.

© Adrian Geoffrey Gilbert, 1991

ISBN 1 873616 00 7

First published 1991

Cover design by John Douet.

Printed and bound in Great Britiain by

Billings Ltd., Hylton Road, Worcester.

The Cosmic Wisdom Beyond Astrology

Towards a New Gnosis of the stars

Adrian Geoffrey Gilbert

To Dee without whose love, support and encouragement this book would never have been written still less published.

CONTENTS

FOREWORD

We live in turbulent times for the spirit of man. After centuries of abuse, we are beset with fears for the safety of our ever more vulnerable ecosystem. The issues of nuclear proliferation, war in the Persian Gulf, poverty and hunger in the third world, unemployment for the masses and rising crime rates have tended to overshadow the utopianism of the sixties. As E.F.Schumacher stated so eloquently in his famous book *Small is Beautiful*, it is not possible to have permanent economic growth in a finite world. In the end resources must run out and with them disappear for ever that elusive quarry 'quality of life' the gaining of which was the purpose of the 'growth'.

For many, particularly young people, the world today seems to have few attractions and even fewer opportunities. Politics of right and left is dominated by economic questions, arguments over ownership and the sharing of the cake. These debates and struggles will become completely pointless when it is discovered that the 'cake' has already been eaten. In any event, these materialistic philosophies offer a very narrow view on life and act as foster parents to the twin demons of envy and greed.

Yet beyond and behind every dark and gloomy storm cloud there still shines the Sun, even though its light be temporarily hidden from our eyes. We should not allow the mundane affairs of the world to keep us forever from seeking to raise consciousness, to find out what it means to be truly human and not just a consumer. More and more people are seeking for the true meaning of life, for a higher purpose or faculty. They are trying to find a deeper wisdom which can give substance and meaning to their existence. However to search is not necessarily to find. How is one to go further than what is commonly taught in schools and universities? The sheer diversity of knowledge, culture, art, science, philosophy and religion would seem to make this an impossible task. How is one to research such an enormity of human experience in one lifetime. The only way that it can be done is to find seams or threads that run through this great tapestry of life and, by following them, to find a common denominator that will unify the diversity of a multifaceted research program. One such cultural seam is Astrosophy, man's appreciation of the cosmos.

Astrosophy literally means 'star-wisdom' and is different from either Astronomy - the scientific study of the heavenly bodies - or Astrology, which is the study of their occult influences upon organic life. Astrosophy, as defined here, is not a science in itself but is more akin to a kind of mental yoga. It is a method of bringing about a higher awareness of nature, oneself and ultimately the great creative power we call God, through the study and contemplation of the macrocosmic world of the heavens. In this context knowledge, 'scientia', is a path and not the goal itself.

Because all men who have ever lived on Earth have done so under the same skies, the Solar System, the stars and the void of space have been man's constant companions throughout history. Right through the ages philosophers have tried to understand the stars and their relationship with man. Astrosophy is concerned not only with the study of the stars but also with the study of man in relation to them and the understanding of how starlore has affected science, religion, art, mathematics, physics, medicine, metrology, architecture and all other fields. We can say that Astrosophy, the 'wisdom of the stars' is the attainment at the end of a long road.

Wisdom (or sophia to give it its greek name) is not the same as knowledge. A man can have knowledge and still be lacking in wisdom. To become wise his knowledge must first go through a process of fermentation. If the gathering of grapes and crushing them to make grape-juice can be likened to the work of the scientist, then fermentation is the work of the philosopher. The quality of wisdom is not itself knowledge but rather consciousness. No amount of know-

ledge can of itself add to consciousness just as no amount
of unfermented grape-juice can be called wine. Yet to make
wine it is still necessary to first crush grapes and to gain
wisdom about a subject it is first neccessary to have
knowledge about it. Books of themselves cannot give
wisdom, even if the knowledge they contain is true and
verifiable. They can, however, give the juice of knowledge
which if properly fermented in the individual may lead to
wisdom.

In trying to study a subject so diffuse and yet all
embracing as starlore, we are immediately up against the
problem of what tools to use. Western science relies almost
entirely on inductive reasoning and empirical research. To
use these sorts of tools all of the time is very limiting as
well as slow. Although truth can often be reached by
logical argument, there are also times when it can only be
touched by its very opposite, by being illogical. In
particular man has the faculty of intuition which is lacking
in any computer. Intuition is not always logical in its
reasoning, yet it can often arrive at meaningful conclusions
in spite of this.

An example of this sort of illogical reasoning is the use
of anagrams. If we take the word 'Earth' and anagram it we
get the word 'Heart'. Logically there is no connection
between these two words, the anagram is simply an
accident of vocabulary and our use of letters. Intuitively the
truth is felt to be quite different. From the similarity of the
two words we can 'feel' a connection. The Earth is like a
heart, it pumps water from the sea into the sky and this
then falls as rain to swell its rivers and irrigate the land
before flowing back once more to the ocean. What is an
illogical deduction intellectually, that these two words have
a close affinity of meaning, is a perfectly reasonable
conclusion intuitively. Equally there are occasions when
what seems logically correct intellectually has no basis or
foundation intuitively. For example, scientists may 'prove'
that there is no such thing as a ghost, yet this would not
convince someone who had seen or felt the presence of a
spirit.

It is this dichotomy that is the source of much misunderstanding in the world today. For many people the cold, dry logic of the scientist is both uninspiring and crude. For others of a more logical disposition, the plethora of unscientific speculations and cranky ideas to be found in 'New Age' literature is an abomination. In order to gain an wholistic picture, we need to go beyond this confrontation and to combine imagination with intellect, fact with fantasy, intuition with logic. The subject matter of this book, what we call here Astrosophy, lends itself peculiarly well to this sort of treatment and this is one reason why it has been written. Its usefulness, however, will depend more upon the reader than the author.

INTRODUCTION

It is with some trepidation that I the author invite you the reader to follow with me the path of astrosophy. I say this advisedly, for there is much in here that may dismay the more orthodox and already I hear cries of 'Heretic!' from pulpit, laboratory and campus alike. Those with a vested interest, with privilege, rank and prestige in their chosen professions abhor new ideas and sometimes even older ones that they have long since neglected. The doctors of philosophy, theology, physics and medicine, the professors of sociology, archaeology, astronomy and architecture, marxists and fascists, bishops and gurus, witches and psychologists are all guilty of a terrible crime: they have perverted truth and hidden the lamp of wisdom!

This book is the fruit of a quest. As to its validity, it must speak for itself. Only you, the reader, may be the judge of its usefulness. It is my urgent wish that it may, as we nudge our way forwards to the twenty first century, cast at least a dim glow in our twilight world. It is presented as a practical and not just a theoretic work. Many ideas included here are intended as hints towards insight rather than over-bold statements of truth. Some elaborations of ideas have been deliberately cut short and others may seem lacking in foundation, in empirical fact. This, however, is an imaginative work and not a textbook of physics. Its desired aim is wisdom rather than knowledge, insight as opposed to proof.

Here in Europe and especially in Britain, we have our own esoteric tradition. This tradition is extremely ancient of which the Christian Church of the last two thousand years is but one flowering. A little research is enough to show that what we think of as 'Christian' revelations are often of much greater antiquity. The roots of western culture are deep and of mixed ancestry and go back not only to

Judaism but also to ancient Egypt, Persia, Greece, Rome, Mesopotamia and the Celtic world. Later parallel flowerings outside of the Christian dispensation have been the Judaic revelation of the Kabbalah and the Sufi tradition of Islam. Within the Christian fold as it were, there have been many more doctrines and sects that those represented by the high street churches of today. These include Gnosticism (with its later developments as the Coptic churches of Egypt and Ethiopia), the Eastern Orthodox Church (with its offshoots such as the Nestorians and Manichaens) and the Catharism of the Albigenses of southern France (the victims of one of the cruellest of all the crusades).

In addition to all of these different religious expressions, old and not so old, there have been various philosophic and religious movements. These were often of a decidedly esoteric character, masked by seemingly orthodox pursuits. Such hidden movements include the Mediaeval Alchemists, the Rosicrucians, the Neoplatonists of the Classical Revival, the masons who built the great cathedrals and the writers of the legends concerning King Arthur and the Holy Grail. Add to this the enormous amount of material available concerning Astronomy, Astrology and Psychology and it is clear that the Western Tradition is in no way impoverished. There is gold enough in our own back gardens to save the necessity of long journeys to the east.

Today the western churches, the supposed custodians of mystical truth, seem to have little interest in the esoteric meaning behind traditional symbols of devotion, particularly those relating to Astronomy and Astrology. They have become preoccupied with social affairs as opposed to spiritual. The churches of today are going through many reforms, changes in customs and are relaxing many of their disciplines in order to draw larger congregations. It is perhaps hoped that by having modern services, playing guitars in church and abandoning fish on Fridays, that the lost sheep will return to the fold. I very much doubt it. For entertainment value the church can offer little competition to the television or disco. If people have stopped going to church it is because it seems irrelevant to their lives, out of touch and above all lacking in mystery. The Catholic Church of thirty years ago, with its Latin Mass, ancient ceremonial, strict disciplines and careful attention to the calendar, still seemed to radiate an air of authority. One might rebel against such an authority but that is not to deny it its reality. Today, like some exiled monarch, the pope wanders the world searching for his lost sheep. He makes pronouncements on everything from arms control to birth control yet his words go ignored by an indifferent public. Religious life in the west has declined to its lowest level since the Dark Ages and the established churches seem powerless to halt the slide.

One reason for this has been the explosive growth in knowledge, in science. Within the last hundred years the atom has been split, men have been sent to the Moon and life expectancy increased dramatically. All of this has been achieved by a new 'priesthood' in white coats. These are the scientists and their acolytes the technicians. When the first doctor did a heart transplant and raised to new life a man all but dead, his miracle was reported in all of the newspapers and his whole profession was able to bask in reflected glory. Now such operations are commonplace. In the modern world of the 1980s, it is to the doctor rather than the priest that people turn with their troubles, for is he not one of a brethren of miracle workers? Alas this is not always so, for great though his science of medicine may be, it can be of no help in answering questions of metaphysics, ethics and the spirit. Indeed even the workings of the human body are only vaguely understood and are often the subject of conflicting theories. The wonder drugs of one generation are considered poisons by the next, the treatments meted out wholesale at one time viewed with horror a decade later.

On the subject of Astronomy science has not been silent either. Probably the greatest symbolic event in the whole history of science was the first landing of men on the Moon. What they brought back with them were some holiday snaps and a few pounds of grubby rocks as souvenirs but it was enough to change forever our relationship with space. Soft landings and flybys to other planets have sent back remarkable pictures and these plus other data have increased our knowledge of the Solar System a thousandfold in a very short time. The one thing they have failed to find any trace of so far is heaven....though they may have found a few hells!

In this authors view it is this changing understanding of the Heavens which is currently the most serious challenge to the authority of the church. The inability of todays theologians to meet adequately this challenge and to re-establish the credentials of the church is possibly the real reason for falling congregations. In a universe of molecules, hot stars, gas clouds, x-rays and above all terrifying emptiness, there doesn't seem to be much room for a heavenly host of angels nor much need for St. Peters keys. It is to this problem that this book addresses itself. Astrosophy, literally star-wisdom, concerns itself with the whole subject of the cosmos and man's relationship with it physically, emotionally, mentally and spiritually. It is not really a new subject but it is one that badly needs re-examining and, if possible, restating.

The study of Astrosophy cannot be divorced from the study of man himself. We are composite creatures of great complexity and with more than one coexistent 'reality'. In the ancient world it was said that man is composed of four parts. These were named as body, soul, mind and spirit. This system of dividing man into four parts or faculties is to be found in most cultures, religious systems and languages. In Latin these were named as *corpus, anima, mens* and *spiritus*, in Hebrew as *nebelah, nephesh, neshamah* and *ruach* and in Greek as *soma, psyche, nous* and *pneuma*.

Unfortunately the divisions of meaning between soul, mind and spirit are blurred almost beyond recognition in Modern European languages, particularly English. However, this system of dividing man was rediscovered and used by the great Swiss Psychologist C.G. Jung. He recognised that our perceptions come from four different sources, which he named as sensation, feeling, thought and intuition. The correspondence here is precise. We can say that sensations come through the body, that is through the ordinary senses, feelings come through the 'soul', the vehicle of feeling, thoughts through the mind, the faculty of thinking and this strange function intuition through what can be called the spirit.

It was Jung's clinical experience that his patients tended to have a bias towards using one or other of these faculties more than the others. There were therefore 'sensation' types, 'feeling' types, ' thinking' types and 'intuitive' types. It would seem that we are all of us biased one way or another and this being so, it must affect our ways of appreciating the cosmos around us. The four faculties of sense, feeling, thinking and intuition lead to different understandings and formulations of knowledge. Practical science is based almost entirely on sense experience, true art has a direct connection with the feelings, philosophy is the product of mental reasoning whilst religion is the expression of the deepest intuition. Any subject can be studied from these four angles and all four are need to give a complete and composite picture of reality. To take into account this natural bias and the fourfold division of man, this work is divided into four parts. For convenience we can label these according to the old system of the four elements as:

a) Sensation (Earth) - scientific observation
b) Feeling   (Water) - artistic expressions.
c) Thinking (Air)   - philosophical speculations.
d) Spiritual (Fire) - mystical insight.

It is, of course, totally impossible to completely isolate these separate functions one from another but this does give some clues as to how the book itself is to be approached. It is not a linear work, even though the pages, chapters and sections come one after the other as with any other volume. In fact the volume itself has been written as a cosmic mandala, which is not an artificial device but in fact the only way that it could truly reflect its subject matter. Each section corresponds with one of the seasons, with one of the four types listed above and with one or another faculty. This introduction and the conclusion are like the outer skin and the inner kernel respectively of the whole volume, a circle which contains four inner circles. Each Book is one of these inner circles, an epicycle, which has its own subjective centre as well as being related to the whole. In each Book there is an introductory chapter followed by several other chapters, so that its structure mirrors the macro structure of the entire volume. The pattern of the volume is the pattern of nature, for each Book is like the limb of a tree which sprouts from the trunk and is like a mini tree in its own right. There is no beginning, there is no end, there is just relatedness and interdependence of ideas.

The core that makes up the subject matter of the book is Astrosophy itself. As this concerns wisdom rather than perception or ideas, it cannot be openly put into words on paper. It is the jewel at the centre and is to be realised in the heart by those who seek diligently. It is understood that different people will find one section or another more interesting or easier to get into than another, this will be because we ourselves are conditioned as types. The first section in particular contains many scientific ideas that may at first sight seem irrelevant. If so skip this section and read the rest, before coming back to it. This is not a book to be read once, memorised and then given to the jumble sale. It is intended as a reference work that will act as an aid to your own fermentation of ideas and it therefore doesn't really matter in what order the chapters and sections are read. It goes without saying that what is written is not the final word on the subject, for these words are only the path and not the goal itself. Therefore do not be over critical of this authors feeble attempt at putting the universe between two covers but rather enjoy any fresh insights and thoughts of your own that may be sparked off by reading this text, for it is these that are in truth the real wine of this vintage.

I

Order in Space

CHAPTER 1
The Metaphysics of Creation

The science of Astronomy has always been one of the most respected of all professions. To be able to look into the night sky and identify constellations, name the brighter fixed stars and note the positions of the moving planets is one of the hall-marks of an educated person. From a simple pair of binoculars to the 200 inch reflector of mount Palomar or the Hubble Space Telescope, there is no shortage of instruments for studying radiations from the heavenly bodies. Such is the prestige of astronomy that no time, effort or money are spared in furthering research into this most remote of sciences.

Given all of this research effort, it comes as something of a shock to discover that in reality the theories concerning the formation of the universe have changed little in thousands of years. The currently favoured 'Big Bang' theory (according to which the universe was formed as a result of a gigantic explosion in the dim and distant past) is also to be found in the Vedas, the sacred writings of India. The Big Bang theory postulates that matter was first concentrated into a tiny portion of the space-time continua under such intense pressure that it had to explode. It is also believed that eventually, under the attraction of gravity all of the particles and stars blown outwards by that great explosion, will once more be drawn back together by the relentless attraction of gravity. The Big Bang theory is a modern creation myth, written in the modern language of the scientist. Comforting as this myth may be from a scientific point of view, it tells us nothing of how the pre-explosionary situation came about. It is a chicken and egg situation. Given eggs, chickens will hatch, given chickens eggs will be laid. But what we need to know is why the universe, the space-time continua, gravity, the Big Bang and everything else came to exist. To this question science has no answer.

When faced with unanswerable questions, the standard tactic of the scientist is to wrap the problem up in a smoke-screen of mathematics, invent some new terminology and pretend that the answer has been found. As a general rule, the more complex the mathematics, the more likely it is that the wrong questions are being asked and the answers fudged. Modern science has developed its own strait-jacket consisting of doubtful hypotheses elevated to dogmatic assertions on the basis of dubious experimentation. The so-called empirical method of science is in reality no such thing. It must be an extremely rare occurrence that a scientist conducts a series of experiments and then seeks to find an empirical solution that would explain the phenomena he has observed. In practice the normal method of science is to invent a theory and then to carry out experiments that will hopefully support this theory.

Science studies nature from the standpoint of cause and effect. By studying the effects it is hoped that the causes may be ascertained. For the sciences of Mechanics and Chemistry, which relate to the behaviour of matter, this method works reasonably well. The possible combinations of atoms and the tension in the chain around a pulley can be computed accurately by applying equations based on known physical laws. These material sciences are not concerned with fundamentals but with secondary results. The laws of Chemistry and Mechanics are a consequence of the way that the material world has already been set up. The periodic table of the elements is as fixed as the rules of 'Monopoly' and can therefore be studied and used with certainty of results. The same is true of the basic laws of mechanics concerning stresses, tensions, leverages, friction and elasticity. Such properties can be measured, weighed and fed into mathematical equations because they are not independent functions but second order phenomena of an already existent world.

Flushed with its successes in the realms of Chemistry, Mechanics and Physics, science has turned its attention elsewhere in pursuit of new conquests. This has had many unforeseen and calamitous consequences because the assumptions which proved so effective in dealing with the subjects of Chemistry and Mechanics have been assumed still applicable in these new sciences. One such glaring example of this misapplication of material laws lies in the field of human biology. Because human beings have bodies, which being made of chemicals must conform to the laws of chemistry, it is assumed that humans are also subject to these same laws. Thus behaviour is attributed to diet or hormonal balance, drugs or secretions. This may be true as regards physical body states but it overlooks the fact that man is more than a physical body and worst of all it disregards the possibility of human will overriding the diktats of Chemistry. The final outcome of such scientific research tends to come out with the flavour of a series of 'nothing but...' statements such as:

'Man is *nothing but* a self-replicating molecular structure'.

'Man is *nothing but* the complex arrangement of DNA ribbons'.

'The evolution of life is *nothing but* the result of a chemical accident in the primordial soup of amino acids'.

All of these statements, though maybe correct from a rigidly physical standpoint, avoid discussion of more metaphysical observations. It may be true to say that the human body is a complex of chemicals held in an hormonal balance. It may be so that the genetic code is held on ribbons of DNA in the cell and that all life has been evolved from a primal soup of chemicals. All of these physical assertions may be correct but they tell us nothing of the purpose of man, of his inquiring mind, of his feeling experience, his will for existence and power of creative invention. To describe man in terms of chemical formulae without consideration of his metaphysical status is a wickedness of supreme folly. It is to pretend that man has no responsibility for his actions, that like some crazy molecule he may continue to despoil the world just so long as his own genes prove themselves fittest for the new desert that will ensue.

In reality, the absurd deductions of human biology that would demote man to the level of the molecule, are not generally accepted at face value. We are, after all, too proud of ourselves and our special achievements to take seriously any theory that might seemingly threaten our status as kings and queens of the Universe. Taken outside of the human sphere, however, these theories have far more appeal. If man is but a machine filled with potent chemicals, is not then the universe also just a collection of molecules, gas clouds and radiant energy in an empty void?

Such a view of space is the starting point for modern astronomers. Following the work of Copernicus, Kepler and Newton, we are now able to describe the motion of the planets in terms of exact equations and to speculate on the nature of the gravitational force that makes this possible. This satisfying outcome has removed the seeming necessity for any metaphysical speculations concerning the Sun and planets. The Solar System having been confined nicely inside a cage of physical equations, modern astronomers treat of it as though dealing with matter in a test-tube. If the contemporary theory of man was folly, this view of the greater cosmos is nothing short of blasphemy. It arises again from the successes in the material sciences of Chemistry and Mechanics and the assumption that the secondary laws of Physics can explain all phenomena both in the heavens above and in man below. It is blasphemous in that there is an implicit assumption that the universe is made of 'nothing more' than matter. To believe this is to deny the reality and independence of such metaphysical qualities as intelligence and creativity. It is another assumption of a misapplied material science to pretend that intelligence can arise out of matter like copper sulphate crystals out of a solution. To believe this is to attribute latently metaphysical qualities to physical matter, which is like saying that shoes can turn into feet.

However, if we deny that intelligence and creativity lie, as it were, locked up in matter, then we must look elsewhere for the source of these powers. Since human beings are the children of the universe and these powers are manifested through humans, then it is reasonable to suggest that these powers are inherent qualities of the universe and are, like matter, made manifest in man. Let us accept then that man is a compound being, a union of physical and metaphysical elements, and in doing so let us also admit that the universe itself is another such union. In looking at man, we see his physical body and can only infer from the signs that he makes just what is in his mind. Similarly, if we look at the physical Solar System, are we not also looking at a physical body, a physical manifestation of a creation with twin parts - physical and metaphysical? The blasphemy spoken of earlier lies not in the appreciation of the physical creation but rather in the denial of the metaphysical.

This brings us back to Astrosophy, for it seeks to go beyond the limits of Astronomy, beyond the physical mapping of stars, planets and moons. and to infer something of the metaphysical qualities of the universe. But this is not an abstract science or philosophy carried on for its own sake. What must be of prime concern is how the metaphysical universe relates to man himself. It therefore is as much a study of man's relationship to the sky around him as it is of the bodies in that sky. This deepens our study and makes it much more interesting, for it puts back 'value' into the cosmos and significance into human life.

CHAPTER 2
Pattern in the Solar System.

We live on a ball that is part of a system of rotating spheres endlessly circling the star we know as our Sun. This in turn is one of a myriad of similar bodies that compose the great Catherine wheel of the Milky Way. There is a harmony, a beauty and a celestial excellence in this music of spinning spheres that has captured the imagination of poets and seers from times of the deepest antiquity. Like the mechanism of some enormous clock, the planets and stars measure out time - day by day, month by month, year by year and epoch by epoch. Can we, whose breath of seventy years is but a moment of cosmic time, honestly suppose ourselves the sole custodians of intelligence and will? Is it given to man alone, this beast of flesh and blood, to experience consciousness and creative power? Is all the outpouring of a trillion suns of no more worth than this, that our telescopes may see and admire a brief flicker of the past?

Surely not! Our ignorance of the cosmos that gives us life is exceeded only by the pride of those scientists who see no more in the bright light of the Sun than the explosion of hydrogen bombs and the steady destruction of a gas cloud. Yet this light, too bright for human eyes, upholds all that lives on Earth. It gives us food and warms our days. Perhaps then we should not be so dismissive of the theory that there could be a purpose concerning such a power in our lives as the Sun.

Victorian scientists made a careful study of the prodigious energy output of the Sun and from this calculated how many tons of coal must be burning each second to produce so much radiation. Today there are scientists who make the same calculations in terms of nuclear fusion reactions. The theoretical physics may have changed but the basic assumption is the same, that the Sun is no more than a giant furnace. Such a concept would have been totally alien to the outlook of ancient peoples, who throughout history have addressed the Sun's power with reverence, awe and often prayer as a divine outpouring of creative light. Yet in our consumer society of ruthless industrial competition and mass exploitation of nature, we have deposed the solar deity from the throne of his temple and consigned him to the factory floor as little more than a source of useful power to drive the mill wheels. The Sun for us has become just another factor in economic calculations and few today believe in its divinity.

Within the Mediaeval Christian tradition the planets were regarded as embodying angelic beings and even today they carry the names of the old Roman gods. Are we right in casting aside old attitudes of treating the Sun and Solar System as being closer than ourselves to the divine whatever that might mean? Many, particularly modern day Christians, would argue that the stars, planets and moons are merely lifeless rocks and dust clouds, scattered pebbles on the beach of space. Yet the evidence exists, if we have but the eyes to see it, that the Earth, her sister planets and the Sun are part of a gigantic plan of creation and not just a curious and accidental by-product of the interaction of material forces. If we cannot see the truth in this then perhaps we are to blame for not looking at the evidence in the right way.

There is an old maxim that 'man is a microcosm of the macrocosm'. We can also see that the phenomenon of 'man' is brought about by the union of the three factors: Form, Matter and Life. If man is made in the image of the macrocosm, then it too should be subject to a comparable, threefold split. If we consider the macrocosmic world of the Solar System then we know that the Sun and planets are composed of matter and that there are energy processes going on between them that are comparable to what we call, in human terms life. The factor that is not generally acknowledged to be of any importance in macrocosmic astrophysics is that of form. Yet the Solar System does have a form and one which is independent of the empirical predictions of atomic physics. If we study the form or pattern of the Solar System, it can tell us much about its function and our own place within that function. Not only that but it can give us some tentative ideas concerning its health and destiny!

It is really quite remarkable that so little interest has been taken in the study of the pattern of the Solar System, for although much is written concerning the physical properties of the individual bodies, little is made of the geometry and dynamics of the system as a whole. In 1618 Johannes Kepler published a book called *Harmonia Mundi*, the harmony of the world. This book contained, amongst other things, his third law of planetary motion. This law, which is founded upon empirical research, states that the speed of movement of a planet around its orbit is related to the distance the planet is from the Sun. The exact formulation of the law is:

$$T^2 = Cr^3$$

Figure 1

where T^2 is the square of the planetary period of rotation around the Sun, r^3 is the cube of the semi-major axis of the ellipse (equivalent to cube of the radius of a circle) in which the planet travels and C is a constant.

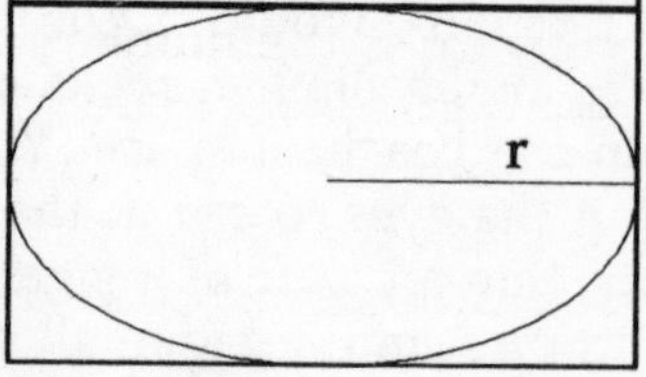

It was one of the greatest triumphs of science when Isaac Newton was able to use his new theory of gravitational attraction to explain the previously only empirical laws of Kepler. However, Kepler's laws of planetary motion and Newton's theory of gravity do not explain why the planets occupy the orbits they do, nor how they came to be in these orbits. Kepler himself tried very courageously to explain the observed planetary orbits in terms of the Platonic solids. For this he has been derided as at best misguided and more probably mystically imbalanced (his interests in Astrology being particularly suspect). Kepler, unlike the majority of modern day astronomers, was searching for the meaning of the Solar System. He believed that it was a *cosmos*, an organised whole, and not just a collection of orbiting rocks. He was searching for a pattern, as one might when viewing a starfish or dogrose, that would explain more about the workings of the system as a whole. The endeavour to do this using the platonic solids may have been futile but his purpose was not. Most later observers have not even made the attempt.

One notable exception was the discovery in 1772 by one Johannes Titius of an empirical law of planetary spacing. This law, now known as Bode's law after the eminent German astronomer who gave it currency, states that the orbital radii of the planets can be calculated from a formula. If we take the distance of the Earth from the Sun as unity (one Astronomical Unit, or A.U.) then the formula is given by the equation:

$$r = .4 + (.3q2^{(n-2)}) \text{ A.U.}$$

where n is the number of the planetary orbit from the Sun and q takes the value of 0 where n is less than 2 or 1 where n is equal or greater than 2.

This equation gives rise to a series of predicted distances of the planets from the Sun which are:

n = 1 (Mercury) r = 0.4   A.U.
n = 2 (Venus)   r = 0.7   A.U.
n = 3 (Earth)   r = 1.0   A.U.
n = 4 (Mars)   r = 1.6   A.U.
n = 5 (?)   r = 2.8   A.U.
n = 6 (Jupiter) r = 5.2   A.U.
n = 7 (Saturn) r = 10.0   A.U.
n = 8 (Uranus) r = 19.6   A.U.
n = 9 (Neptune) r = 38.8   A.U.

For these nine orbits the rule is obeyed fairly rigorously in terms of actually observed and measured distances in

A.U.'s and gives rise to the following table.

planet	prediction	actual
Mercury	0.4	0.39
Venus	0.7	0.72
Earth	1.0	1.00
Mars	1.6	1.52
Asteroids	2.8	2.90
Jupiter	5.2	5.20
Saturn	10.0	9.55
Uranus	19.6	19.20
Neptune	38.8	30.10

That this series shows some anomalies should not detract from the extraordinary fact that there is a series at all! Indeed, as often happens in such cases, the apparent anomalies in the series point to other interesting hypotheses concerning the structure and history of the Solar System.

It may have been noticed by the attentive reader that the planet Pluto has so far been left out of this scheme. By applying the formula, we would expect to find it at a distance of approximately 77.2 A.U. from the Sun. In fact it occupies an orbit that falls far short of that at roughly 39.5 A.U., which is close to the predicted orbit for Neptune. Because Pluto has a highly eccentric orbit, there are times when it is actually nearer to the Sun than Neptune. This fact, as well as its relatively small size (it is smaller than our Moon) have inclined astronomers to the view that Pluto was at one time a Moon of Neptune. This does seem a likely explanation for its not obeying Bode's Law.

A second anomaly is the case of Mercury. The equation as given earlier is $r = 0.4 + (0.3 \, q2^{(n-2)})$. In the case of Mercury, it is a requirement that the second term, that is the bracketed function, should take on the value of zero. Hence the value of q has to be zero, whereas for the other planets it takes the value of 1. This points to the fact that Mercury is to be considered as a special case and in fact there are other reasons for thinking this, which will be discussed later. Indeed Mercury appears to be more like a Moon of the Sun than a planet in its own right.

There is however a third major discrepancy. According to Bode's Law, we would expect to find a planet in the space between Mars and Jupiter at a distance from the Sun of roughly 2.8 A.U.. In fact what we find is the Asteroid belt. Though many astronomers prefer to talk about debris left over from the formation of the Solar System, the pattern of Bode's Law suggest that this 'debris' is what remains of a former planet that once occupied this orbit. Some clues as to the fate of this planet that once orbited between Mars and Jupiter, can be gleaned if we study the pattern of the Solar System further.

The planets fall into three distinct groups. Firstly there are the small, rocky planets: Mercury and Pluto, secondly the terrestrial planets: Venus, Earth and Mars and thirdly the gaseous giants: Jupiter, Saturn, Uranus and Neptune. We have already discussed the possibility that Pluto is not really a planet at all, in the true sense of the word, but rather an escaped Moon of Neptune. Perhaps we can now be more specific and list certain characteristics that we can say are typical of planets. These could be laid out as follows:

1) A planet orbits the Sun at a distance predictable from Bode's law.

2) A planet has a spin of its own about its own axis that is independent of its rotation about the Sun.

3) It has an atmosphere.

4) It has a magnetic field of its own.

There is one further characteristic that is usual but not universal and this is the possession of one or more satellites of its own. In the case of the Earth, of course, this is the Moon.

If we look at the planetary orbitals, it is not unreasonable to see parallells between the way that this system is organised and the way that electrons are arranged in shells around the nucleus of an atom. The science of chemistry came of age with the tabulation by Mendeleev of the periodic table of the elements. According to the atomic theory, the atom has an internal pattern, electrons being arranged in 'shells' around a central core. There are only seven of these shells and they are not exactly alike. In fact they increase in complexity as we go down the series, to the point where elements with electrons occupying the outermost shell are too complex to be stable for more than very short periods of time.

The shells are really patterns of energy levels and can be thought of as something like the contour lines that describe a hill on an ordinance survey map. If we continue this analogy further, we could imagine a 'Sisyphus' rolling a heavy boulder up the hill-side. Whilst he is pushing the boulder up the slope, he is constantly struggling against gravity and the boulder will have a tendency to roll back down again should he for one instant let go of it. However, if he is lucky enough to find a ledge, a level part of the hill, then he can push the boulder onto this and it will be quite stable while he takes a rest.

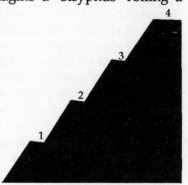

figure 2

We can imagine a mountain with a series of ledges or plateaux on the way to the top (as in figure 2) and each of these ledges would be possible resting places. If we were to draw a two dimensional map of the mountain using contour lines (like an ordnance survey map), then the lines would be close together where there is a steep

figure 3

slope and further apart where there is a ledge (figure 3). The ledges would represent allowed, stable, energy states where Sisyphus can take a rest. However, between the ledges there is extreme instability and he would have to keep working hard to stop the boulder rolling away. As an alternative diagrammatic representation, we might decide to leave out the contour lines and simply to draw in the ledges, all at their right distances from the central axis of the mountain (figure 3).

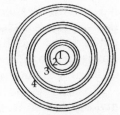

figure 4

In the case of pushing a boulder up a mountain, the ledges get progressively smaller as we ascend until eventually we must reach the peak. However, let us now look at the reverse case, where the boulder is being pushed not up a mountain but rather up the inside of a deep, bowl-shaped depression. The shelves will now be in the reverse order as they go up the sides of the bowl (figure 4).

This diagram begins to look remarkably similar to the picture we have of energy states in the atom. The shelves correspond with the electronic shells and the bottom of the depression with the central nucleus. Just as the boulder is only stable when standing on one of the shelves, so also the electrons in an atom are only able to take up stable energy states which correspond to the shell positions. This is referred to as quantisation of energy states. The electron can only have exact, integral amounts of energy when inside the atom. The allowed energy states of the electrons in the atom are characteristic and electrons take up or give out energy in bursts, not gradually.

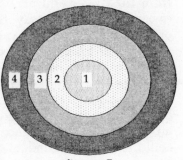

figure 5

Figure 5 is also very similar to the model we have of the Solar System, the ledges corresponding with planetary orbits. Now, gravitational theory on its own would suggest that planets can exist at any distance from the Sun provided they travel fast enough to keep obeying Kepler's third law. It therefore seems to be something else that is quantised, not gravity, which causes the planets to tend to take up the pattern dictated by the empirical Bode's Law. What then can it be that gives order to the arrangement of planetary orbits if it is not gravity?

To attempt an answer to this question, it is helpful to make recourse to a fresh model and again to probe for the truth by analogy. Let us now imagine a large circular stadium with a steeply banked track, perhaps something like the old Brooklands racing track. If we were to drive a car around the track, then the faster we travel the higher we can climb up the banking. If the surface of the track is of uniform tarmac, then the energy required to pull against gravity and move up the banking progresses at a steady rate. This linear progression, if we were to study it mathematically, would give rise to an equation similar in form to Kepler's third law.

Imagine now, however, what would happen if the tarmac were not uniform but rather striped in bands of varying surface friction. It could then be that certain bands were much easier to drive along than others, that staying in these bands gave more stability and required less attention from the driver and allowed for optimum running of the car. We could then say that the track was quantised as opposed to uniform and cars would tend to move from one stable band to another, spending as little time as possible on the bands in between. What this means is that having now introduced an independent, variable factor, i.e. friction, the behaviour of the cars is no longer a simple relationship between gravity and speed. If we knew nothing about the tarmac and the importance of its friction qualities, then we could not, as independent observers, guess the reason why the racing cars tended to stay only on certain specific bands of the track. It would, for us, be a matter of empirical observation inexplicable within the context of our knowledge of dynamics.

If we now return to studying the structure of the atom, there are more analogies to be found. However, for the benefit of those readers who have not studied chemistry, wave mechanics and atomic physics, we must first digress a little and discuss some basic atomic theory. We have already made brief mention of the currently accepted theory whereby it is stated that electrons in the atom are held in shells. It must now be mentioned that these shells are not all the same as one another. Each shell within the atom contains one or more 'orbitals'. These orbitals are not actually orbits, like those seen in the Solar System, but rather three dimensional geometric shapes in which the electrons are held like peas in a pod. Each orbital is capable of holding a maximum of two electrons and the shells within the atom differ according to how many orbitals they in turn have available.

The first shell has only one orbital available for filling with electrons and this is of the simplest, *s*, type which has spherical symmetry. The second shell has four orbitals, one of which is an *s*, the rest of them being *p*'s. These last are shaped like dumbbells and are at right angles to one another along the three axes of space. The third shell has nine orbitals available which include one s, three *p*'s and five *d* orbitals. These last are really quite complex in their geometry, the details of which need not concern us here. The fourth shell has not only all of these but seven *f* orbitals in addition, making fourteen in all. The fifth, sixth and seventh shells have other orbitals as well as those listed above, but they are not actually met with in practice except for in highly excited states of matter, so we need only consider the first four types.

As we go down the order of the shells, so the potentiality for exhibiting varieties of chemical properties is increased. The first shell, which has only one orbital, gives very rudimentary chemistry, that of the hydrogen atom. The second shell begins displaying new properties which are seen chemically in the behaviour of such elements as Carbon, Oxygen and Nitrogen. The third shell allows for not only the types of behaviour characteristic of the last two, but also that of the so called transition metals including Iron and Copper. The fourth shell doesn't add very much chemically speaking to what has gone before but gives rise to a whole family of elements, known as the Lanthanum series, whose properties vary hardly at all one from another.

In summary it can be said that the development of electronic shells, from simple to complex, is what causes the full range of chemical phenomena on which the natural world rests. By way of analogy this development of shells and associated properties forms, as it were, a model with which to study the structural physiology of the Solar System. Without wanting to push the analogy too far, we can see something of the same progression of properties of the planets as we can chemical properties as they relate to the activity of specific orbital types.

The first period of the periodic table is extremely primitive. This shell contains only one orbital and can therefore only contain two electrons at most. It can be compared with the orbit of the planet Mercury. Just as in Chemistry the first atomic shell has no p orbitals and therefore only exhibits the fundamental spherical structure of the s orbital, so we can say that the orbit of Mercury is governed only by the first part of the Bode equation ($r = 0.4$). It could be a fundamental aspect of the developing Solar System that the first member of the Bode series only displays the constant part of the equation and not the variable part.

Similarly, if we take the second planet Venus, we could compare this with the second period of the periodic table. In this case the second, variable part of the Bode equation is in evidence. We also see that the planet itself seems much more developed. Whereas Mercury is a rocky body, seemingly with little or no atmosphere, in fact more like a Moon, Venus has a dense atmosphere and a highly developed weather system. In many respects Venus is the sister planet of Earth, they are very alike though for humans it would be an impossible environment in which to live.

The next planet from the Sun is Earth. Again we can see a more developed and differentiated stage has been reached. The third shell in the atom is that which is capable of giving rise to what are known as transition metals. We can see that with the Earth, the third planet, there are similar developments. The first of these is the presence of a Moon. The second is a greatly increased axial rotation, which in turn gives rise to a much stronger magnetic field. Not only is there an atmosphere but there is also an ocean, out of which emerged the first life forms. To us this is the central event in creation but we should try not to let our own self-interest prejudice a more objective look at the Earth's position in the order of the whole system.

With the planet Mars and then the Asteroid belt, the pattern of development seems to be broken. From Mercury to Earth there seems to be a steady increase in size and importance of planetary structure. With Mars we are faced with a dilemma, why does it seem so undeveloped in relation to the Earth? At this juncture it is better to leave further discussion of Mars and to return to it later after we have discussed the other planets beyond the Asteroid belt.

The first of these is the great, giant Jupiter. It is by far the largest of all the planets and contains more mass than all of the others put together. Its diameter is over eleven times and its magnetic moment is nineteen thousand times that of the Earth. It is now known that Jupiter emits more radiation than it receives from the Sun and if we remember that it has at least thirteen moons of its own (including the four large Galilean satellites visible with an ordinary pair of binoculars), then it begins to look not so much like a planet but more like a mini star system in its own right. Jupiter also rotates extremely rapidly on its own axis, for although it is large in comparison with Earth, the Jovian 'day' is much shorter than our own. In fact it lasts for only nine hours and fifty one minutes, with the result that there is tremendous atmospheric disturbance in the thick cloud belts that surround it. It would seem that whereas the chief feature of the Earth is the maintenance of an environment that enables life to exist on the planetary surface, the

characteristic of the Jovian system is size and the multiplicity of differing lunar environments that exist within its
system.

Conditions upon Earth appear to be more similar to
those prevailing on the moons of Jupiter than the planet
itself. One could imagine spacemen landing on the surfaces
of Mars, or Mercury or even Venus but to land on Jupiter
would be impossible. This great planet would crush and
destroy immediately anything as fragile as a spacecraft.
Even to be near Jupiter would be to put life in peril given
the strength of its magnetic field and intense radiation. It is
therefore not unreasonable to see Jupiter as a body midway
between planet and Sun.

With Saturn, the next planet out from Jupiter and the
last of the so called inner planets, we have a shrinking in
size and seemingly of importance compared with Jupiter.
The mass of Saturn is less than a third that of Jupiter,
though its diameter is over four fifths that of its giant
neighbour. Therefore Saturn is less dense than Jupiter and
in fact it would float on water. What is particularly special
about Saturn is the development of its ring system. Recent
space missions have revealed that both Jupiter and Uranus
have tenuous ring structures but nowhere else in the entire
Solar System is there anything to compete with the
complexity and beauty of the saturnine rings. This planet,
like Jupiter, has many moons and one of these, Titan, is as
large as a small planet.

Saturn is the seventh member of the Bode series and it is
the last that can be seen with the naked eye. Together the
two great gaseous giants would seem to hold a special
place within the Solar System. Just as it would appear that
the Earth is in the middle of the most favourable orbit for
the processes of carbon life to take place, so these giant
planets seem to be in the most favourable orbits for
planetary growth and the formation of moons and ring
systems.

Beyond Saturn lie Uranus and Neptune. These two
planets are roughly the same size and remarkably similar in
many ways. They are much smaller than Jupiter with

masses of only five and six percent of that planet and they are composed mainly of different elements. These planets are cold bodies with liquid ammonia, methane and ice present in their mantles. Uranus is peculiar in that it has an extremely tilted axis, almost at ninety degrees to the ecliptic, and it rotates on this axis in reverse direction to the other planets. It has a family of at least five moons and a faint ring system reminiscent of Saturn's. Neptune is slightly larger than Uranus. It has at least two moons, with Pluto as a likely contender for a third at one time. In some ways Uranus and Neptune resemble the terrestrial planets, notably Venus and Earth, but in other ways they are much more like the great giants Jupiter and Saturn.

If we compare planetary masses, then there is a curve of growth from Mercury to Earth and a curve of decline from Jupiter to Pluto. Since the two planets Uranus and Neptune appear midway in size between the terrestrial planets and the gaseous giants, then we would expect to see their counterparts in the inner solar system occupying the orbits of Mars and the Asteroids. Yet, in fact, Mars is a disappointingly small body. It has a mass not much more than a tenth of that of the Earth and a volume of only fifteen percent. It has a thin atmosphere, mainly composed of Carbon Dioxide and a very weak magnetic moment. Mars resembles the planet Mercury more than any other and does not seem to represent a transition stage from the Earth to the giant planet Jupiter as we might have first expected.

Between Mars and Jupiter lies the Asteroid belt. This is a region containing a large quantity of debris and planetessimals, some of which have been named and charted. There are asteroids in other parts of the Solar System but they seem to be most common in this region - just where we would expect to find another planet. Looking at this debris one instinctively feels that this is the remnants of a lost world, destroyed either by some momentous internal explosion or shattered by a collision with some other body.

It is not an unreasonable hypothesis to believe that during the early stages of the formation of the Solar

System, the mechanics and regularities of movement of the various bodies were not as stable as they now appear to be. We can imagine that if there had been a planet present between Mars and Jupiter, then it would have had several moons. Thus, what could have happened was that an instability in the orbit of its moons led to a collision between it and the parent planet. If we stop thinking of planets as being like hard billiard balls and instead picture them as they really are, like eggs with a 'yoke' of molten metal and rock at tremendous pressure, then we can better imagine the effect of a mantle tearing collision. This would explain not only the disappearance of the planet from its orbit but also the heavy cratering on other planets and moons of the Solar System including Earth, Mars and Luna. Since Mars would have been the nearest neighbour of this exploding planet, it is likely that it would have been the one most badly affected by the explosion of its neighbour. If we consider that the planets are not just a random collection of rocks but rather, as is the hypothesis of this chapter, an organised structure whose parts are interdependent, then it is not unreasonable to suggest that the disruption of the planet Mars went further than a simple bombardment of its surface and radically affected its possibilities of evolution.

Planetary development would seem to entail such functional properties as axial spin, magnetic moment, containment of atmosphere by a magnetic envelope and the formation of a system of moons. On all of these counts in addition to mass and volume, the Earth would appear to be a far more evolved planet than Mars. It is clear that at one time Mars did have a denser atmosphere and even surface water. Now, however, these have all but disappeared. It is really as though the life has gone out of Mars and that what we are looking at is a planet that has died. As for the two 'moons' of Mars, these misshapen potatoes look much more like trapped asteroids than genuine moons. They can hardly be counted as evidence of advanced Martian development.

To complete this brief survey of the Solar System, let us

now list all of the fragments of evidence and scientific analogy that have been put forward in this chapter and see whether there is any definite picture that emerges.

1) We can now say with some justification that Kepler was right in looking for a spatial relationship to explain the position of the orbits of the planets. Had he discovered it, Bode's Law of planetary spacing would have supplied him with the evidence he needed to back up his own intuitions.

2) It is also clear that this law of planetary spacing cannot be explained by gravitational theory alone. There must be some independent factor, as yet unexplained by science, that dictates the positioning of major planets.

3) There is a curve in the development of functions, size and importance that tends to grow to a peak with Jupiter and then to tail off again with the outer planets.

4) Since each planet is different from each other, it would appear that there is variety of environments within the Solar System, for what purposes we do not know.

5) There would appear to be evidence to suggest that we live in a Solar System which has been damaged at some time in the remote past. At least one planet would seem to have been destroyed and others, particularly Mars, have been severely affected as a consequence.

The pattern that emerges from all of these deliberations is one of a Solar System with value. A special collection of bodies in space, which are patterned according to a definite spatial order and which experience processes of growth, development and even death and decay. This surely is a Solar System of greater worth and interest than the cold, dry and dusty void so beloved of astrophysicists. Let us therefore embrace this new understanding, for in putting value back into the cosmos we are also putting it back into ourselves as we live out our lives on the surface of this marvellous, blue planet.

CHAPTER 3

Living Worlds

The concept of a planet 'dying' does not fit very well into the framework of current, scientific theory. We can imagine the biosphere of the Earth being so badly polluted (by nuclear warfare for example) that all life on the planet's surface died. However, this is quite a different proposition from saying that the planet itself had died. Since we don't tend to think of the Earth as having a life of its own in the first place, the concept of death in this context would seem at first sight to have no meaning.

Life is the greatest of all mysteries, for by its unseen power it creates life-forms. The body of insect or elephant is not just an inert mass of chemicals but rather a highly organised and specialised production plant. All organisms are able to manufacture elaborate molecules and cell structures from the base material of food. It is this ability, this inherent capacity for the transmutation of food into complex structure that is the hallmark of life, the difference between the quick and the dead.

Biotechnology, along with data processing and tele-communications, is regarded as one of the sunrise industries. However, even simple organisms are capable of manufacturing complex organic compounds and often this is done far more cheaply and effectively in the belly of a worm than inside an expensive piece of chemical plant. The new industry of biotechnology is a form of chemical farming that makes use of the skills inherent in these simple organisms. Living cells not only manufacture complex molecules from food and air but many of them are also able to collect energy from sunlight. Almost our entire economy depends upon coal and oil deposits that were laid down many millions of years ago by the same processes of photosynthesis observable in any field or wood today. Without the continuous work of Mother Nature, there would be no food to eat, no wood with which to build and no flowers to brighten our gardens. Our debt to her is enormous though seldom acknowledged.

It seems there is a hidden power to life, a quality that transcends ordinary chemistry and physics and which stands in defiance of the devil of entropy. This power of life lies in the realm of metaphysics and cannot be explained by the ordinary laws of the laboratory. Life is purpose seeking and not the result of blind evolution or chemical accident. An organism will, for example, evolve special cells to manufacture a particular hormone or enzyme needed for some other remote part of its being. Such activity implies connectedness of its parts and the creative intelligence of a supreme chemist. We may think of this intelligence as resident, though subconscious, inside the organism itself or we may regard it as being external in the form of a creative deity. What we cannot sensibly do is to deny the activity of intelligence in the directing of life. It always takes intelligence to make bread out of stones.

Many scientists would be prepared to accept that the phenomenon of life as seen in the myriad of plants, animals and most especially in the human race, cannot be explained in terms of simple physics. What then of the Earth itself, is it alive ? Before attempting to answer this question, it would perhaps be worthwhile to look at some of the current theories concerning the formation of the universe.

Up until the early part of the twentieth century, it was assumed that the atom was the smallest particle of matter that could exist. The researches of such eminent scientists as Marie Curie and Ernest Rutherford shattered forever this comfortable assumption. It was proved that the atom is indeed itself composed of small particles, a heavy nucleus of protons and neutrons and an outer sheath of electrons. Furthermore, by splitting the atom it was discovered that the nucleus could be divided and hence one element could give birth to another. A further development was the discovery that not only could the nucleus be divided but smaller nuclei could be joined together to make larger ones, a process of fusion rather than fission. In both cases it was discovered that nuclear reactions release huge amounts of energy which can be used either destructively in bombs or usefully in power stations. Whilst electricity generated by the fission of Uranium atoms has been a fact of life for several decades now, scientists have long been pursuing their own Holy Grail, a workable fusion reactor. The difficulties inherent in this work have seriously clouded our views as to what is happening in the natural world around us. There is a tacit assumption that because fusion reactions, when conducted in the laboratory, require high temperatures and pressures, they could not normally be taking place within the Earth. It is assumed that in nature such reactions could only occur at the heart of hot stars such as the Sun.

According to current theories, stars begin life as a cloud of Hydrogen gas which then condenses under the pull of gravity to form a densely packed body. When this packing becomes tight enough, atomic nuclei are forced together and fusion reactions are initiated. Eventually, after millions of years, when the Hydrogen has nearly all been turned into heavier elements, the star explodes and scatters these elements into space. These then find their way into other star systems and are incorporated into the structure of planets such as the Earth.

As so often happens with modern science, this theory of star and planetary formation takes no account of any possible metaphysical reality and assumes that all the natural phenomena of world creation can be explained in terms of the same old laws of gravity and atomic physics. But what if the theory is wrong? What if the Sun and other stars are not breeding grounds for heavy elements? How could planets such as our own be formed if there were no mineral enriched, interstellar gas-clouds? Needless to say these questions are never asked, for the 'theory' has taken on the form of 'dogma' and is seldom even questioned.

We have seen how, in the case of Chemistry, biological

life-forms are able to perform complex chemical reactions by using some unique property of their own called 'life'. When we try to duplicate these reactions in the laboratory, we need all manner of expensive equipment to provide the right special condition for the reactions to work. Even then the yield is often very low, whereas life processes generally produce much higher yields and don't require high temperatures and pressures. As was said earlier, life-forms have a purpose orientated approach that causes them to organise their own environment and to change its chemistry to suit themselves. If this is true in the micro world of living organisms, could this same ability be present in the macro world of a whole planet?

There is still much that we do not understand about planets, especially what goes on internally. We tend to think of our planet, Earth, as a solid ball, a slightly flattened sphere of hard, impermeable rock. Nothing could be further from the truth, for not only is two thirds of the surface covered by water but the crust, (itself in constant, crunching movement) covers a mantle of rock which because it is at extremely high pressure, behaves in very strange ways. The crust at its thickest, is still only about twenty five miles deep. In contrast the planet's diameter is over seven thousand nine hundred and twenty miles. Little wonder then that our knowledge concerning the Earth's core is so limited.

We are well acquainted with the phenomenon of life as manifested on the Earth's surface but what if the core also has analogous properties involving the organising power of some intra-terrestrial life-force? What if the Earth is actually able to condense cosmic energy to make matter and then to bind lighter atoms like Hydrogen to make heavy ones such as Iron? We would then be talking of a 'growing' Earth and not a world which is more or less static from the atomic point of view. We should not judge this to be an impossible proposition. It is the latent conservatism of science which has sought to banish nuclear fusion to the stars, for modern science is against 'Life' as an independent force. It will not bow down to the superior power of a metaphysical reality whether this be called God, the Life-force or simply the living nature of the Earth and Solar System.

Let us hypothesise that we take our existence within a living world of matter and not the dead carcass of an inert planet. Let us suppose that Mother Earth is very much alive and is herself evolving. Our views on astronomy then take on quite a different colour and our interpretations of the phenomena around us will be quite different also. Within the Earth itself we can see a material circulation going on. The typical geological processes involve the formation and destruction of mountains, plains and valleys. The continents, which are no longer believed to be stationary, are now seen to be rocky platforms which float on a sea of fire. At the edges of the Pacific Ocean the continents collide and matter is forced back down into the Earth's mantle. Meanwhile, in the Atlantic the opposite process is occurring and matter is spewing up to form the Atlantic ridge. These are only glimpses of the sort of activity taking place within the interior of the Earth and they involve prodigious amounts of energy. Can we honestly say that it is impossible for nuclear changes to be taking place? Could not the Earth's spin and its magnetic field have a hand in this? These are lines of research that desperately need to be followed up.

Magnetism in particular appears to play a much larger part in astrophysics than hitherto realised. The largest planet, Jupiter, has a colossal magnetic field associated with it, whilst that of the Sun appears to stretch into space beyond the orbit of the farthest known planet. In the previous chapter we considered an example of cars racing round a banked track and used this as a figurative analogy for the movement of planets in their orbits. In the example it was suggested that there could be certain bands of low friction on the track which would make for greater stability of driving. If this were so, then the track would be quantised into favourable and unfavourable bands. The favourability of bands would be determined not so much by speed and gravity but rather by friction.

If we now look at the Solar System, it can be seen that

an analogous situation exists. The planets each travel in an orbit predictable from Bode's Law. This behaviour cannot be explained by gravitational theory alone but must be the result of the working of some other quantised force which is comparable to the friction on the racing track. The most likely candidate for the honour of being this force is magnetism. One of the curious characteristics of magnetic fields is that they have shape but seemingly no substance. If we shake iron filings around a bar-magnet, then they will take up the shape of the magnetic field even though this field is invisible to the human eye. Now we know that the Sun has a powerful magnetic and gravitational field associated with it that extends far out into space. If the Bode series means anything, it would seem to indicate that this field is banded, it has a pattern to it.

Within the micro world of the Hydrogen atom, it is well known that the shell structure of electrons originates from the quantisation of energy states. The energy level of an electron inside an atom goes up or down in fixed jumps. It cannot be just any value but must correspond exactly with the pattern of allowed energy levels inherent in the shell structure of the atom. The pattern of the shells and the orbitals available to the electrons is a function of the basic pattern of the atom. It is present, like a flight of stairs, even before the orbitals are filled with electrons. In a similar way we can say that the Solar System has a set of exact orbits that agree with its fundamental structure. These are magnetically quantised according to the Bode equation and only within these basic orbits can true planets be formed.

Scientific observation also reveals that magnetism, electricity and electromagnetism go together like tea, milk and sugar. We can see that the Earth is radiated constantly by light, or electromagnetism, from the Sun but not so apparent is the way in which it is affected by the Sun's magnetic field and any associated electrical affects. It could be that in this lies the secret within the Earth's core. Perhaps in some way the centre of the Earth is able to act as a dynamo and transformer. The interaction of the Earth's metallic core with the Sun's magnetic field could be what

causes the Earth to spin, which in turn would cause the
secondary magnetic field of the Earth. This magnetic
envelope, the magnetosphere has a profound affect upon
the atmosphere and both protects the surface of the planet
from deadly radiation and contains the edges of the
atmosphere to prevent seepage or loss of material. The
process of magnetic induction and transformation into spin
and secondary field is a type of energy transformation
analogous to photosynthesis.

In the last chapter it was also pointed out that the
planets are not of uniform size or development. To
understand the reasons for this variation we need to turn
again to the story of Sisyphus rolling his bolder up the
mountain. We have considered how, although the boulder
is all the time being attracted downwards under the force
of gravity, there could still be certain ledges available
which allow him to take a rest. The structural presence and
the strength of these ledges is able to counterbalance the
force of gravity so that the boulder can be laid to rest while
he takes a nap. There is now a further consideration to be
taken into account. Suppose that he has now left a boulder
on a ledge, leaves this one and now goes off to fetch
another. If nobody moves the boulder and it is left on the
ledge for a long enough period of time, then plants will
begin to grow on it. However, just what does grow will
depend upon the altitude at which he left it and the
availability of water, sunlight and plant seeds.

By analogy we can see something of the same process in
the Solar System. We can think of the planets as having
each been left on the equivalent of a ledge. The planet
Mercury, which is closest to the Sun, would seem to be a
barren desert. Whereas Earth lies at an ideal 'altitude' for
organic life to flourish. Looking further out into the system,
it can be seen that Jupiter is most favourably located for
Moon formation as is Saturn for ring development. In this
way we can argue that planetary development is brought
about not only by the quantisation of the Sun's magnetic
field but also by the balancing of Solar proximity (and
hence light) with ambient galactic radiation and influence,

(a sort of cosmic 'water').

Taking all of the hypotheses discussed in this chapter together, we can arrive at a new theory for the formation and development of the Solar System. The story begins with the nascent Sun (though how it itself came into existence remains a mystery). As it accumulates mass, the embryonic Sun develops a strong gravitational field. This field is uniform in its affect and spreads out evenly in all directions and has the tendency to pull all matter towards the Sun's centre. When a critical mass is reached, a magnetic core is formed and this has the affect of setting up a magnetic field that is not uniform but rather quantised into bands of strong and weak influence. Within the quantum zones planets are formed, though this may not happen uniformly. We may speculate that this is not just a matter of the working out of physical laws but that it involves the direct intervention of a metaphysical power analogous to 'life'.

By processes of internal fusion and the condensation of energy into matter, the planets are able to grow. This growth continues until a point is reached when they too begin to spin and to manifest a strong magnetic field of their own. With the help of this field the planets are able to establish their own satellites, the moons, in stable orbits. This then provides for a multiplicity of structural environments in the same fundamental orbit about the Sun. The development, and hence appearance, of a planet and its associated moon system would seem to depend upon the following factors:

a) Distance from the Sun.
b) Ambient radiation from the galaxy.
c) The age of the planet.
d) Accidental influences.

Taking these factors into account, we can hazard the following deductions concerning our Solar System.

1) The order of ages of the planets (assuming this is related to size) must be Jupiter, Saturn, Uranus, Neptune, Earth, Venus, Mars, Mercury, Pluto.

2) The planet that once orbited between Mars and Jupiter was, when it was destroyed, probably about the same age as the Earth is now.

3) Mars seems to be in a state of arrested development, in which case it may be very much older than its size would suggest.

It must be admitted that this theory for the formation and structure of the Solar System is highly speculative. Even so, it is necessary for the accepted theories of science to be challenged from time to time with radically different hypotheses. This is particularly so when, as at the present, it has become so materialistic in its outlook. There is nothing shameful in invoking metaphysics and incorporating the 'Life Force' as a factor in a theory of world formation. Life is after all our prime reality and should be given a central place in any theory of creation. Our experience of life as manifested through Carbon chemistry is probably too narrow to properly understand its full metaphysical potential and implications. The life of our planet is expressed through its biosphere but that does not mean that life necessarily stops there. Perhaps within the Earth and indeed inside the other planets too, there is an organising power at work, which when active leads to growth and when static gives way to decay. If this is the case, then we are justified in calling the planets living worlds and should modify our attitudes accordingly.

CHAPTER 4

The Astronomy behind Astrology.

Before going any further into this subject, it is worthwhile making a preliminary study of the fundamentals of Astronomy. When we look up into the night sky, the heavens above appear like a vast dome with the stars as points of light projected upon it. Wherever we stand on the Earth's surface, this dome of stars is above us, so that conceptually we can imagine that just as the Earth is a sphere, so the heavens form a greater sphere around it. This sphere, which is referred to as the 'Celestial sphere', has an equator corresponding to a projection of the Earth's and two poles which are the continuation of our own north and south.

Although in reality it is the Earth which spins, it appears to us as if the sphere of the heavens rotates about a fixed axis linking the north and south celestial poles. The north pole of the celestial sphere is easy to find as it is close to the star Polaris in the constellation of Ursa Minor (the small bear). This star always stands in the same place, thus marking for us the direction of true north. The south pole is harder to find and cannot be seen from the northern hemisphere but it lies in the constellation of Octans.

In order to facilitate the study of terrestrial geography, we have given names to the various continents, oceans, mountains, deserts, rivers and plains that make up the surface features of the Earth. In a similar way, names have been given to the various groupings of stars that make up the 'continents' of the celestial sphere. These groups of

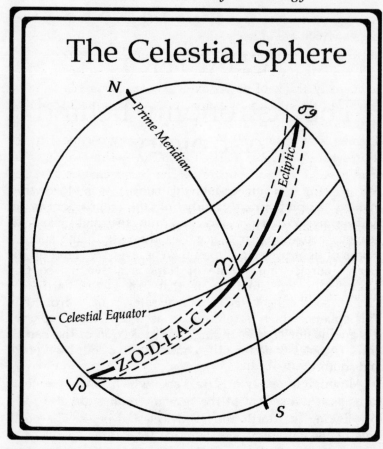

The Celestial Sphere

stars are known as constellations and are currently 88 in number. Most of them are named after mythical characters in Greek mythology such as Perseus, Hercules, Andromeda and Orion. Others are identified with fabulous beasts such as Draco (the dragon), Pegasus (the winged horse) and Cetus (the sea monster). There is also a third group of constellation with names of a less personal nature such as Crater (the cup), Argo Navis (the ship Argo) and the river Eridanus. Although some constellations (notably Orion the hunter), do bear a close resemblance in shape to the subject after which they are named, it must be admitted that most

do not. It would appear that these constellations have
names which are either symbolic in some other, mythological way or have been acquired purely by historical chance.

The Earth travels around the Sun in a fixed orbit, which
we usually think of as an extension of the Sun's equator.
However, the Earth is not upright in relation to its orbit. It
appears to be tipped over at an angle of 23 and a half
degrees and rotates like an inclined gyroscope. In the
course of a year, the Earth makes an entire circuit of its
orbit around the Sun but for us the perspective is reversed
and it is the Sun which seems to traverse a path through
the sky. If the Earth were standing with its axis of rotation
perpendicular to its orbit, then this pathway would
correspond with the celestial equator. However, because
the Earth is tipped over, the Sun appears to us to follow a
different course through the stars marked by an imaginary
circle on the surface of the Celestial Sphere called the
Ecliptic.

To understand this, imagine that the Celestial Sphere is
like a rubber ball. If we draw a horizontal circle around the
middle of the ball, this correspond to the celestial equator.
We can then draw a second circle, also with its centre
corresponding with the centre of the sphere only this time
inclined to the first at an angle of 23 and a half degrees.
This circle represents the Ecliptic. In fact the two circles
would be like interlocked bangles that cross each other
twice. Because of this, half of the Ecliptic lies inside the
northern hemisphere and half is in the southern.

The Sun appears to move along the circle of the Ecliptic
by roughly 1° of arc per day. This means that it spends
half of the year in the northern hemisphere and the other
half in the southern. When it crosses the Celestial Equator
(as it must do twice a year), day and night are of equal
duration. These are the so called equinoxes and they mark
the start of spring and autumn respectively. When the Sun
reaches its extreme positions of latitude, either its most

northerly or most southerly position on the celestial sphere, we have the other two major turning points of the year called, respectively, the summer and the winter solstices.

All stars, with the exception of planets, occupy fixed positions relative to one another. The latter (with the exception of Pluto), circle the Sun in almost the same plane. This means that when we view the night sky from the Earth. we can only ever see planets on or around the region of the Ecliptic. In fact they are always at most 7° north or south of this line and this means that the area through which they travel is marked by a narrow band that also extends 7° north and south of the Ecliptic. This region of the sky is called the zodiac and the constellations which lie across its path on the celestial sphere are called signs of the zodiac. There are twelve of these signs which divide the zodiac into twelve, unequal portions. Because of this, the planets and luminaries can be said to pass through the signs as they make their way around the zodiac.

One of the reasons why astrology is often dismissed as mere superstition is because of a widespread misunderstanding concerning the 'influences' at work causing the phenomena under investigation. It is a commonly held belief that to be born with the Sun occupying a particular sign of the zodiac means that the stars making up that sign have a special relevance to the person born 'under' them. This is an understandable mistake given the confusion of terminology employed by astrologers. It is made even more absurd because conditions in the heavens have changed greatly in the period of roughly two and a half thousand years since our current zodiac was formulated. This astrological zodiac is really a clock face and was only ever intended to be used as such in reckoning the astrological influences prevalent upon the Earth at any given time.

In fact if one looks at the actual signs, the constellations that make up the zodiac, they are of unequal size. Some, such as Libra and Cancer, are really rather small and inconspicuous whilst others such as Pisces and Aquarius, though consisting of rather dim stars, are extremely large. Still others, notably Leo, Taurus and Gemini are both fairly large and bright. In fact it is neither the size nor the brightness that counts, for astrologically the stellar zodiac is of only symbolic importance. If stellar radiations were what matters, then one would expect the greater influence to come from such constellations as Canis Major, Orion, Aquila and Ursa Major all of which contain bright, powerful stars of the first magnitude. The true importance of the zodiac lies much closer to home than remote stars and galaxies. In fact most astrologers are hardly concerned at all with the actual stars that make up the zodiac, what they study is the Sun-Earth cycle of interactions.

When the Ancient Greek and Egyptian astrologers put together our current system of astrology some two and a half thousand years ago, the movement of the Sun through the signs of the zodiac was taken as the basis of the psycho-philosophical system they wished to expound. This system concerns the vegetative cycle of the Earth and not the processes going on in deepest space. To understand this we must consider more closely the situation in which we live. For us there are three principle time cycles that are of the greatest importance and significance for our lives. The first of these is the daily cycle, which as everyone knows is caused by the rotation of the Earth on its own axis. The second is the monthly orbiting of the Moon that gives rise to its phases and the third is the annual cycle of the Earth about the Sun, our year. All of life is profoundly affected by these three cycles, not least mankind. Any attempt at formulating a system of astrology must in the first instance take into account these three cycles.

Measured in days, the synodical period of the Moon from one new Moon to another is roughly twenty nine and a half days. The length of the solar year is roughly three hundred and sixty five and a quarter days. hence there are approximately twelve and one third lunations to one solar year. It follows from this that the natural way to divide up the year is into twelve portions, one for each Moon or month. Because the division is not exact, when we wish to make a calendar a choice has to be made as to whether the lunar or the solar cycles are to considered as more important. The Gregorian calendar as used in western countries is predominantly solar in its perspective but there are lunar calendars still in general use, most notably the Moslem. Astrologically things are somewhat simplified, for both cycles can be considered separately and charted accordingly.

The start of the astrological year is normally taken to be the day on which the Sun enters the northern hemisphere, that is to say the day on which it crosses the celestial equator from south to north. This day is known as the spring or vernal equinox. At the time when the zodiac was fixed, it happened that the position of the Sun on this day of the year was in the sign of Aries, the ram. This sign was therefore taken as marking the start of the year and the zodiac was split up into twelve exactly equal portions roughly corresponding with the twelve constellations of the zodiac and starting from this point of 0° of Aries. Thus it is we have the familiar pattern of spring beginning with Aries, summer with Cancer, autumn with Libra and winter with Capricorn. For several hundreds of years this system was a quite accurate representation of astronomical facts but then owing to the precession of the equinoxes, reality and philosophy began to slip apart.

It was mentioned earlier that the Earth spins on its axis like a gyroscope and that it is tipped away from the perpendicular axis of its orbit by 23 and a half degrees. This is not, however, the whole story for its movement also has a slight wobble, like a gyroscope that not only leans over but whose axis of rotation itself changes direction and drifts round and round in circles. At present the axis of the Earth (and therefore by extension of the hypothetical celestial sphere) is pointing almost directly at the star Polaris, the star at the end of the tail of the little bear. At about 3000 B.C. this axis was pointing at the star Thuban in the constellation of Draco and in 12000 A.D. in should be pointing near the star Vega in the constellation of Lyra. It completes a circle and returns to pointing at the same point at approximately twenty six thousand year intervals. This period of twenty six thousand years marks a Great Year and it is a time cycle of very great importance astrologically.

The affect of this wobble in the Earth's rotation is not confined to the direction in which its north-south axis is pointing but also determines the relationship between the celestial equator and the ecliptic. As the direction of North changes, so this point of intersection moves backwards around the ecliptic. At the time of the ancient Greeks, the Sun crossed the celestial equator as it went into the sign of Aries. This is no longer true, for the point of intersection of the ecliptic and equator has now slipped back by one sign. Throughout the Christian era, the spring equinox has taken place with the Sun in the sign of Pisces, the fish. It is now almost out of this sign and moving into the sign of Aquarius, the water bearer. This is what is meant when it is said that we are moving into the age of Aquarius.

Unfortunately it means that Astrology is now a science which is out of sync with itself. In relation to the solar cycle, a person born during the first thirty days of spring is still said to be an Aries but the Sun is no longer to be found in the constellation of Aries at this time but rather in the sign of Pisces! At first sight this seems nonsensical and indeed it would be if we were to consider the Sun as acting as a sort of magnifying glass that focuses the 'rays' from the stars in the sign it is travelling through. If such were the case, then we would have to conclude that an Aries person is really a Pisces, a Taurus is an Aries, a Gemini a Taurus etc. etc.. However, we don't need to be too concerned for what we are really saying when we call a person an Aries is that they are born within the period of the first twelfth of the year. We are concerned with the ever changing Earth-Sun cycle and not with the background stars that make up the clockface.

All this makes sense as far as the Sun-Earth cycle is concerned but the movement of the planets through the signs of the zodiac would seem at first sight to be of little scientific significance. Whilst it is true that astrologers set great store on what signs the planets are occupying, this may seem a rather artificial preoccupation as these signs do not correspond with the constellations of the same name. It must be remembered that because of the precession of the equinoxes, a planet in say Taurus is actually to be found travelling amongst the stars of Aries when physically viewed in the night sky. The solution of this paradox may be found if we make a more careful examination of just what is meant by the zodiac. Although the spring equinox has precessed backwards by over 30° since the time when the constellations were given their present names, we still call the first month of spring Aries and measure the zodiac from that point. The spring equinox occurs always at the time when the Sun seemingly crosses the celestial equator from south to north. This point marks one of the two junctions of the ecliptic and equator and is referred to as 0° Aries.

It is because the orbit of the Sun, the ecliptic, is not the same as the celestial equator that we have markedly different seasons. After the Sun has moved into the northern hemisphere in spring, it carries on day by day going further and further north until it reaches the point of its most northerly latitude, 23 and a half degrees, on the day of the summer solstice. It then begins moving south again, passing the equator in a reverse direction at the autumn equinox and reaching its most southerly latitude on the winter solstice, a few days before Christmas. The affects of this cyclic activity are very obvious in the way that they are reflected in the pattern of nature on the Earth's surface, for the Sun is the source of light, power and life as far as this world is concerned. When the Sun is in the northern hemisphere the days grow longer and the nights shorter. The further north it travels, the longer it is visible in the sky, the more direct are its rays and the hotter the days become. Heat is accumulated in the atmosphere during the spring and summer months and gradually lost again during autumn and winter. The more hours of sunlight per day and the more direct its rays, the more intense the heat. Conversely, the fewer the hours of light and the lower it rises in the sky, the colder the atmosphere becomes.

The Sun cycle is easy to see and appreciate and it is directly related to the zodiac. What is not so easy to see is how this same zodiac could be relevant to the planets. What we have to remember is that with the exception of Pluto, which may not even be a true planet, they never stray very far from the ecliptic. The important consideration here is what is called the orbital inclination. This is the amount that the orbital plane of a given planet differs from the orbital plane of the Earth. Apart from Pluto, the maximum discrepancy occurs with the orbital plane of Mercury which is 7° to the ecliptic. This means that none of the major planets is ever more than 7° above or below the ecliptic and in fact they are usually within a degree or two. As a result of this, it can be said that the declination (number of degrees north or south of the celestial equator) for any planet is closely related to its position within the zodiac. This means that the length of time the planet spends above the horizon depends upon it position in the zodiac. It is therefore fairly accurate to say that any planet reaches its maximum declination when it is in Cancer and minimum in Capricorn. The discrepancy timewise is never more than a few weeks and often only a few days.

It has been pointed out that it is because the Sun shines for longer and more directly at this time of year, that summer is warmer than winter. If we accept for a moment that planets also emit an 'influence', then it should be at its strongest when they are at their maximum, northern declination and at its weakest when they are at their most southerly. If we hypothesise that the Earth's atmosphere is able to absorb and store radiations of the planets in a way analogous to the storage of solar heat, then there will be a steady build up of a planet's influence as it moves north and steady decline as it goes south.

There are of course other factors that need to be taken into account if one wants to use this reasoning to make accurate predictions concerning planetary influences. First of all there is the question of the planet's proximity to the Earth. Obviously if a planet is in the part of its orbit that is further away from the Earth, then even if it is high in the sky its influence may be weaker than when it is in close proximity. Also, because planetary luminosity appears to be mainly due to reflected sunlight, then the size of illuminated planetary crescent could also be a factor that needs considering. A 'full' Mars may be stronger than a 'half' or 'new' one for example.

Far more research needs to be done into the whole subject of planetary influences if they are to be properly understood. What has become clear from recent research is that the position, in relation to the horizon, of the planets at birth has a profound influence upon psychological disposition and may give a clear indication of what will be the future interests and therefore most suitable type of employment for a person. This work needs following up, for it could lead to a sensible system of career guidance, something very lacking in our schools today. All in all there is no reason to dismiss astrology as superstition. As we have seen in this chapter, it is at root founded upon clear scientific principles relating to the ebb and flow of cosmic cycles. The study of harmony, vibration and the recurrence of cyclic phenomena is surely the very heart of modern science. Given it's pedigree and relevance to the modern world, it would be surprising if astrology were to remain the neglected half brother of astronomy for very much longer. On its renaissance our very futures may depend.

CHAPTER 5

Cycles of life.

To understand the meaning of the zodiac, it is necessary to see that what is being studied is a repetitive cycle. Any cyclic process can be easily split into four phases and therefore given diagrammatic representation by the typical pattern of a so called 'sine wave' as in Figure 1.

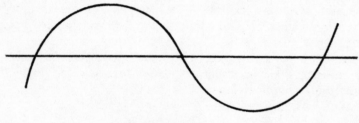

Figure 1

The wave grows (phase 1) from the origin O, reaches a peak P and then declines (phase 2). It then passes below the origin, becomes negative and continues to decline until it reaches a negative trough T, which is the mirror image of the positive peak. Finally it begins to ascend again (phase 4) back towards the origin and the start of a new cycle. This fourfold cycle is what is called Simple Harmonic Motion (SHM). It is the underlying process behind many natural phenomena such as the vibrations produced in guitar strings or organ pipes, light waves, the rotation of a body about a fixed point, the pitch and roll of a ship or the bouncing of a rubber ball. It is therefore not surprising that the orbital cycles of the planets, the Sun and the Moon are all typical SHM's and can be represented diagrammatically as sine waves.

If we follow the motion of the Sun along its imaginary path, the Ecliptic, then it is easy to see that the four fundamental phases which make up its SHM cycle correspond to the four seasons. Each season contains three signs of the zodiac. The first sign marks the start of that season, the second the middle and the third the termination.

There is, however, something more that needs to be considered, for the annual cycle causes the rhythm of nature, that is the periodicity of all the specialised processes we think of as life. The cycle of nature, though repetitive, is not completely passive. It involves inner processes and a dynamism which can be compared with the working of a car engine. Normally such an engine runs according to a four stroke principal. On the first stroke there is an intake of fuel and air mixture, the second stroke is one of compression, the third is the power stroke and the fourth expels the waste gases. This cycle involves something more than just a vibrating motion, it concerns the transformation of energy. In this case the transformation is from the potential, chemical energy of the fuel to the mechanical motion of the piston. In a similar way, the process of nature through the four seasons is not just that of a simple spinning top but is also a process of transformation.

There are indeed many of these processes that go on in nature but the simplest to see is the one which we call photosynthesis. All of life depends upon the ability of plants to absorb sunlight and to use this energy to manufacture carbohydrates. The light from the Sun is transformed in several different ways, the simplest of these transformations is into heat. The radiant energy from the Sun is not of itself hot since heat is a property of physical matter and not a wave function. It is when radiation is absorbed by matter that it is transformed into heat. There are also other photo-chemical reactions, similar to those used in photography, that occur when sunlight interacts with the chlorophyll in the leaves of a plant. However, photosynthesis does not just depend upon sunlight but also on other vital ingredients, in particular the presence of water. Now, it may seem obvious to say it, but if the Sun shone continuously all day and every day on all parts of the Earth's surface , then the temperature of the Earth would rise to the point where all its water would be vaporised and life would be impossible. To keep the balance of nature we require night as well as day, dark as well as light, cold as well as hot.

We can say then with some accuracy that the process of photosynthesis is one of transformation that works by the interplay of hot and cold. If heat is generated from sunlight, so in a sense cold is generated by darkness. The cycle of the year is the alternation of light and dark. Darkness and hence cold being the pre-existent state of the Earth, heat being caused by the absorption of sunlight. Where too much heat predominates, then a desert like the Sahara is formed. Where the excess is cold, then nature becomes the realm of the ice-queen, as it is for example at the polar ice caps. It is a great mistake to only see the year as the growth and diminishing of light. It is also the growth and diminishing of dark, which is itself an independent force of equal importance, though of opposite function, to light.

During each and every day there is a period of light and a period of darkness. Whilst the sum of the two must always come to twenty four hours, the balance between them shifts throughout the course of the year. We should in fact plot not just one graph (the sine wave of light) but rather a double graph which shows symbolically the shifting balance of the two alternating curves of light and dark as they weave their way through the year (Figure 2).

Figure 2

At the latitude of London, England (51 1/2 degrees north), there are never more than roughly 16 1/2 hours of either light (at the summer solstice) or of dark (at the winter solstice). This represents a maximum split of roughly two thirds to one third. Further north the extremes are greater, until a point is reached at latitude 66 1/2° (the arctic circle) north of which there are periods of the year when the Sun either doesn't set or doesn't rise at all. The shifting balance between light and dark is not just an astronomical curiosity, it also has a profound affect upon human consciousness, moods and psychology. As anyone who has spent a winter in Scandinavia will know, the hardest thing to come to terms with is not the cold, severe as this may be, but rather the long periods of darkness. This heightens the awareness of the dream side of life, the unfathomable depths of the unconscious psyche and this can either bring wisdom and self-knowledge or deep depression and despair. This is the reason why there is such a high level of suicides amongst Scandinavians.

Even at more temperate latitudes, the cycle of the year is of profound significance psychologically. Each month, or sign, lends itself particularly well to some specific type of activity. It follows, therefore, that if we make use of this cycle and plan our lives accordingly, then it will give added impetus to our endeavours. Conversely, if we work against the cycle, then our work can be as futile as growing tomatoes in winter - and as difficult. As with any cycle there is a degree of arbitrariness as to what is to be considered its beginning. Our calendar, which is Romano-Christian in origin, is generally taken as starting near the winter solstice, January the first being ten days after December the twenty second. In Roman times it was customary to take March as the first month of the year, which is why we have the Latin names September (seventh), October (eighth), November (ninth) and December (tenth) for months which by our reckoning should be ninth, tenth, eleventh and twelfth respectively. The Roman custom of starting the year in March is also the reason why the extra leap year day is put at the end of February, for this would have been the last day of the Roman year.

There are other calendars, for example the Hebrew, which start the year at the autumnal equinox. In many ways this is a better place to begin for it marks the end of the harvest. Each month of the year there is appropriate work to be done and by following the zodiac from Libra right around the zodiac and back to Virgo, we can plot the tide of human affairs. There is therefore a very practical side to Astrology and to this end the following notes on the signs may be of some use.

☆   **Libra (September 22nd to October 23rd.)**

This is the time of the change of the balances, it ends the period of growth and fruition and begins that of dormancy. With Libra the balance of life-force moves inwards once more. The period of summer, the 'silly' season is over and one returns to a state of greater seriousness, self-consciousness and psychic awareness. Often at this time the precious summer seems no more than a dream, a happy memory of absurd behaviour, indiscretion and wasted money. What looms ahead is the long autumn and winter months which will demand frugality and inner resources. Libra is a time for bringing as much peace and harmony to oneself as possible in preparation for the darkness that is to come.

☆   **Scorpio (October 23rd to November 22nd.)**

The Scorpion brings the death sting and autumn proper takes hold at this time of year. Almost everything in the garden either dies or goes into hibernation with the first frosts of autumn, which usually occur under this sign. Traditionally it is the time to kill off all excess livestock whilst they are still fat. Psychologically the time of Scorpio is often one of pain and inner conflict as one is made to face the consequences of the past cycle. The time of Scorpio is fatalistic and can be compared with the moment when one receives marks in an examination. At that moment it is no longer possible to change anything, yet the results of the test will decide exactly what is in store for the coming year or even longer. As with any test there is a criterion for success and failure. Too much of the latter will mean one cannot go on further. In this sense Scorpio is linked with the law, for true justice is a life and death issue and allows for no bending of the rules to suit political convenience.

☆   **Sagittarius (November 22nd to December 22nd.)**

This is the time for planning and projecting ahead. Physically one is still bound to the present, which is one of moving towards the depths of winter but mentally one should be looking ahead towards the following spring and summer. It is easier to be clear headed at this time of year and the experiences of the past cycle are still very much in mind as one plans ahead for the future. If one receives unfavourable judgement in Scorpio, then Sagittarius is the time to pick up the pieces, whatever they might be, and see what can be done with them. It is also the time of advent in the Christian calendar, a period of preparation leading up to the great feast of Christmas.

☆   **Capricorn (December 22nd to January 20th.)**

This is the time when the ground plan for the next cycle is begun. Having thought ahead in Sagittarius, one now begins the steady plod in Capricorn. Farmers traditionally ploughed their fields and trimmed their hedges at this time of year in preparation for the next season and in readiness to sow new crops. In most countries it is still the start of a new financial year, a time to put the past, with any associated remorse, behind and to begin again with a new cycle. The great feast of this period is of course Christmas. Symbolically Christ, the new light, is born in the dark, in a stable. Similarly much of the work of Capricorn is done indoors, working on accounts, financial forecasts, buying in raw materials and new equipment etc.. Unlike Sagittarius it is not a time suited to imaginative thinking, particularly after the twelve days of Christmas. Rather it is one of tedious but necessary g.ound work without which no serious project would ever succeed.

☆   Aquarius (January 20th to February 19th.)

Inevitably whenever one begins any project there are going to be unforeseen difficulties and problems ahead - no matter how good the planning. The time of Aquarius represents the period in any project when new ideas of how to do things come to us. It is the time when necessity demands invention. Usually it is just when a project is floundering that we suddenly get new inspiration and fresh insights. The pressures of necessity and contingency are required to galvanise the deeper levels of creativity within us. Often this will only happen when things are at their darkest, at their lowest ebb. The time of Aquarius is in the middle of winter, during the cold months of late January and early February. Used wisely this can be the most inventive time of the year and give rise to something quite new that will manifest in the following spring and summer. It is also the time when we are most prone to depression, hence the high suicide rate at this time of year.

☆   Pisces (February 19th to March 21st.)

Pisces is the last of the winter signs. Physically it can be a time of great stress, particularly when the winter has been a hard one. Each of the so called 'mutable' signs, that is Pisces, Gemini, Virgo and Sagittarius represent transition periods between two conditions or seasons. they are times of preparation and adjustment. During Pisces we are preparing for the spring and this can be as stressful as the day before starting a new job, going to a new school or preparing for a first date. The autumn and winter months are, in a sense, private. That is they are more related to our own personal, inner world of thoughts, feelings and intuitions. During the spring and summer months we are drawn out of ourselves to be once more on stage and we become more removed from the unconscious world within that harbours our creativity. Pisces represents a final stock-taking before stepping out again into the hurly-burly.

☆   Aries (March 21st to April 19th.)

This is the first sign of spring, when the Sun crosses the ecliptic and moves once more into the northern hemisphere. At this time libido shifts from the inner, subconscious world back to the outer world of the ego. Traditionally this is the time when we begin spring cleaning and open the doors to rooms which have been left unoccupied throughout the long, cold months of winter. Aries is a time of great vigour which needs to be controlled carefully or accidents are liable to happen. Properly harnessed, this extra energy can give a huge boost to any project we are trying to get off the ground. However, success will depend upon how well we have prepared for the spring during the previous winter months.

☆   Taurus (April 20th to May 21st.)

This is a time of great joy as spring is now in its prime. During Taurus whatever has been planted, be it flower or weed, will grow vigorously and identification of which is which can be difficult if not impossible. One must carry on regardless and assume that preparations have been adequate, for there comes a time in any project when we must stick with what we have already planned and stop altering the blueprints, otherwise nothing will ever become concrete. Any mistakes in our plans must now be lived with and can only be ironed out in the following cycle, for during Taurus it is sensible to let nature take its course or there will be no harvest to gather in autumn.

☆   Gemini (May 21st to June 21st.)

The time of Gemini, just before summer proper, is probably most people's favourite month. At this time the days are long and growing longer, the plants are green and growing vigorously and there is a period of calm before we need think about harvesting. At this time of year most people are feeling relaxed and looking forward to the summer months. This makes them more open and communicative than they might otherwise be and more willing to share their feelings with strangers. This is probably the best time of year to take a holiday, for it is the time of children and games. Any schedule which does not leave time for holidays, recreation and family life is imbalanced and needs altering.

☆   **Cancer (June 21st to July 23rd.)**

At this time of year the Sun reaches its maximum northerly latitude and there is still the prospect of at least two hot months ahead. Agriculturally this leads to fears of draught, an ever present risk if the summer is exceptionally hot. Thus care has to be taken to preserve the balance of water and fire. People are psychologically at their most extroverted in summer and this can lead to callous, rude and egotistical behaviour. It is easy under such conditions to lose sight of matters of greater importance and for individuals to act like cancer cells in the human body. Summer warmth also brings out the mosquitoes and other parasites, which can be quite a problem at this time of year. Sources of trouble should be pin-pointed and if minor dealt with promptly, just as if swatting a fly. If they are too large for this sort of treatment or there is a risk to the venture as a whole, then wait for the time of Scorpio.

☆   **Leo (July 23rd to August 23rd).**

This is the second sign after the summer solstice and is therefore midway through the season. The period of Leo is generally the hottest time of year, for by now the Earth has had time to warm up. At the start of this month occur what are called in Europe the 'dog days', the time when the Sun rises close to the star Sirius, the dog star. During this period food rots very quickly if left exposed and everything seems to go off. Drought is an ever present threat and work

can be a real exertion, especially if there is an early harvest
to be brought in. It is therefore a time of struggle, for
developing will-power and not allowing projects to stag-
nate or be halted by the power of the Sun.

☆ Virgo (August 23rd to September 23rd.)

This is the last month of the summer and is traditionally
the time of harvesting. It marks the end of the cycle that
began twelve months earlier in Libra and it is also nine
months after Sagittarius, the time of planning. A poor
harvest can mean bankruptcy or even starvation, so the
work of Virgo is to get in as much of the harvest as
possible, to make hay while the sun shines. Even manufacturing companies have to do this, for products only have a
limited lifespan before they are either outmoded or the
market becomes saturated.

This then completes the cycle, which now begins again
with Libra. The theory of astrological correspondence
between people and the sign under which they are born is
directly related to this natural cycle of change. It is believed
by astrologers that people are particularly responsive to the
influences of their own time of year, especially their own
birthdate. Unscientific as this may seem, most people
believe that there is something to astrology and are well
aware of what is their own sign. If we take the zodiac and
describe the twelve processes of the signs with single
adjectives, we can arrive at single word descriptions for
people born under those signs. These would be:

Aries	Dynamic
Taurus	Strong
Gemini	Playful
Cancer	Crafty
Leo	Wilful
Virgo	Prudent
Scorpio	Remorseless
Sagittarius	Intuitive

Capricorn   Diligent
Aquarius   Inventive
Pisces   Helpful

It would be quite wrong to believe that only people born under a certain sign are capable of acting in the way described by these adjectives, for a truly whole person aims to be able to adopt the correct attitude for whatever task is to hand. However, it remains true that we all have special aptitudes and talents and it could be that these are in part determined by our astrological birth-sign. It is certainly important to realise that the characteristic behaviour and talents associated with each of the twelve signs is not arbitrary and not essentially linked with the stellar constellations after which the signs take their names. It is rather a consequence of the alternating cycle of light and dark that is the driving force behind nature and which in turn affects man not only in body but in mind also. If science refuses to accept the validity of astrology it is because it is looking for rays and forces from the stars. The real astrology is neither of these things, it is the science of man in nature, the relationship of symbol, cycle and psyche. This is the secret hieroglyph of the stars. How this secret has found expression in our cultural values will be the subject matter for the next section.

II

Astronomy and Culture

CHAPTER 1

The Cosmic Role of Art.

Interesting as the scientific study of astronomy is, it will always remain incomplete, for it cannot include any of the subjective feelings which are evoked by the experience of cosmic phenomena. To describe a sunset in terms of refracted light and atmospheric impurities may be scientifically correct but misses the real point about sunsets, their emotional intensity. Where science ends art must begin, for it is the duty of the artist to represent as accurately as he can the intangible qualities of feeling that lie beyond the range of scientific instruments. Indeed one measures the value of a civilisation by the quality of its art.

Today we tend to think of the artist as something of a Bohemian, one who is able to cock a snook at convention and either paint or sculpt as the mood takes him. This type of art may well be valid but often it becomes so personal that only the artist himself can grasp the meaning of his work. Having invented a language of his own to suit his own tastes, he is unable to communicate his ideas to a wide audience, though many may pretend to understand. Indeed so abstracted has much of modern art become that often the artist himself is totally mystified by his own work and cannot give a coherent account of what he was trying to achieve.

Whilst artists have probably always enjoyed a special place in society, their talents earning the respect of their less gifted patrons, they have more usually had to work towards a definite purpose. We generally think of such monuments as the Taj Mohal, the Parthenon and the Pyramids of Giza as possibly the greatest works of art to come down to us from the past. Yet they themselves are only the fruits of the cultures that bore them. The pyramids speak directly of ancient Egypt as the Parthenon does of

Classical Athens. for they were not built as a personal whim but to express commonly held beliefs concerning life, science and the universe.

The work of the artist in antiquity was to show in a meaningful way the underlying unity behind diverse phenomena. Art in this sense is not limited to music, architecture and painting but uses the whole of life as its medium of expression. Thus in a truly civilised as opposed to barbaric community, religion, politics and economics are conducted in an 'artistic' way and therefore brought into correspondence with the greater pattern of the whole. High civilisations such as those of ancient Egypt and China endured for thousands of years because they were founded upon the bedrock of a universal philosophy. This was given artistic expression through every department of life. We, in contrast, live at a time of decay. The forms and expressions which upheld civilisation in Europe for nearly three millennia have lost their vigour. At the same time our scientific knowledge of the world is increasing daily and is not easily assimilated into our culture.

There have been enormous changes in Europe since the time of the French Revolution. The Austro-Hungarian, French, German and Russian royal houses have all lost their thrones and given place to other forms of government. Eastern Europe, never a very happy place since the time of Genghis Khan, has slid into an abyss of repression, from which it is desperately struggling to emerge. Meanwhile the West debauches itself in a frenzy of inflation, financial double-dealing, greed and the self-inflicted malaise of drug abuse.

If Europe seems changed then in the third world the effects of new knowledge and technology have been devastating. What were once stable, if backward, countries are now disaster areas. They have been destabilised by the impact of modern medicine on infant mortality rates, the development of huge new cities and above all by the inability of their own indigenous cultures to meet the challenges of the modern world. Bereft of faith, identity and sense of purpose in a world robbed of its spiritual heritage, the people lapse into a state of alienation and shock. Little wonder then that there has been an explosion in crime both against the state (terrorism) and the individual (robbery, murder and rape). Such statistics are a clear measure of a steady slide into barbarism.

If we would halt this slide, then art must return to its prime function of integrating the individual with the whole, of bringing a higher meaning into the tasks, customs, life and environment of the people. The prime assets of the artist throughout the ages have always been on the one hand his inventiveness and ability to be topical and on the other his knowledge of symbolism. Consciously or unconsciously we deal with symbols almost all of the time, whether they be words, logos, pictures, shapes or motifs. What is not commonly realised is that our culture itself is built upon a foundation of very particular symbols relating to astrological ideas. In this way there has been much wisdom handed on from generation to generation that might otherwise have disappeared entirely.

As the world is changing so much of this wisdom is disappearing too, leaving us with a sense of vagueness and vulnerability. Without a coherent cosmology as expressed through the reassuring presence of artistic devices, our lives seem fragmented and meaningless. It is probably true that as this is a time of change, many of the older symbols of our culture are no longer relevant and are for that reason losing their force. It will probably be several generations before a new set of cosmic symbols are worked out to take their place. In the meantime it is worth re-examining our inheritance to make sure that we don't lose the essence along with the form. We must grasp the esoteric meaning of our culture from its artistic expression before both perish.

CHAPTER 2

The Copernican Revolution.

The Renaissance, which for convenience we may date from Columbus' historic voyage to America in 1492, heralded the dawn of modern science. Throughout the period of the Middle Ages and before knowledge, both spiritual and temporal, was concentrated in the same hands, those of the church with its ordained priesthood. The rediscovery of America by Columbus (there is now abundant evidence that the Vikings had sailed to Nova Scotia centuries earlier) toppled the simplistic notion that the Earth was flat and set the scene for the dramatic revolution in ideas that was to follow.

In 1543 Copernicus published a book called '*De Revolutionibus Orbium Caelestium*' (concerning the revolutions of the celestial spheres). This was the first major work on Astronomy for about 1400 years and not surprisingly it caused a storm. Whilst it is very likely that Ptolemy of Alexandria and other earlier Egyptian astronomers knew that the Sun and not the Earth is the central body of the Solar System, this knowledge was considered to be esoteric and was never published openly until the time of Copernicus. There are two likely reasons for this censorship. Firstly the prime concern of such astronomers as Ptolemy was Astrology and to the astrologer the physical rotation of the planets about the Sun is of minor importance compared with their apparent motion around the Earth. It is this motion after all, which marks the ebb and flow of planetary 'influences' as experienced by human beings. Knowledge of the actual mechanics of the Solar System may have been kept as a trade secret, as part of the mystery of the craft. A second reason for censorship may others. It is scarcely surprising that the church tried to suppress this knowledge for as long as possible. By displacing the Earth from its exalted position of centre of the Universe and showing that it is in fact only one of many revolving bodies, the story of the creation, fall, redemption and eventual resurrection of man would seem to have become but a small sideshow compared with the great drama of galaxies, nebulae and star systems.

Prior to Columbus and the Copernican revolution, it was still academically sound to believe in a material heaven somewhere beyond the clouds and a hell under the flat Earth. The new knowledge gained through science has rendered such simplistic Astrosophical models untenable. Without a material heaven to go to, such ideas as the resurrection of the body at the last trumpet call begin to look rather suspect. Faced with such contradictions, the church has backed off from the whole subject of Astrosophy. Instead it condemns Astrology and ignores entirely the subjects of space science and material evolution. In doing so the exoteric, or outer, teaching of the church has become curiously ambivalent and self-contradictory regarding the purpose of life on Earth. The church, particularly the Church of England, has become less and less spiritual in its outlook and more and more secular. For many clergymen the afterlife has become of much less concern than the social struggle of the classes here on Earth. Other sects have become more and more fundamentalist in approach, such groups interpreting the bible word by word and, when this disagrees with the findings of science, taking refuge behind a smokescreen of dogma and bitter rhetoric. The affect of both these attitudes has been to drive a larger and larger wedge between what might be called the scientific outlook and the religious.

In spite of all the changes in liturgy inaugurated by the Vatican Council and Church Synod, in spite of the abandonment of Latin in the Mass and the updating of the Common Book of Prayer, congregations continue to fall. To the young particularly the church looks more and more out of place in the modern world. One reason for this decline, have been fear about the affect such knowledge would have on the Astrosophical notions held at that time by both church and people.

In certain respects the work of Copernicus has parallells with that of Charles Darwin. The latter's *'Origin of species'* shattered for all time the cosy notion that God literally created the universe in six days and rested on the seventh. There are fundamentalist groups in America and elsewhere who still hold to a literal interpretation of Genesis but they are now in the minority, they are as distant from the mainstream of accepted wisdom as is the flat Earth society. The majority view of creation, shared by academics and clergy alike, is that the Earth is of far greater antiquity than any literal interpretation would allow. Indeed we have physical evidence from the fossil record of species that existed many millions of years before even the most primitive of humans walked the Earth.

Most people today regard the first chapter of Genesis as at best a piece of poetry. However both the literal interpretation and the poetic miss the real point and meaning of the story. Genesis is a mystical book and it was written in a language which is symbolic. It was intended to be read, used and interpreted by an instructed priesthood who had themselves been taught the esoteric meaning of the text. Its style is that of a dream whose contents have to be explored, considered, pondered and cross-referenced before they will give up their inner truths. This form of story telling, of history as myth, was quite normal in the ancient world even if it is a style that seems alien to the modern intellectual.

The Fundamentalists fight the Darwinists on the issues of the formation of the world and the origin of species because it seems to them that the old world order of bible, church and state is threatened by the new wine of exact science. New knowledge can be hard to come to terms with when it undermines the philosophical structures on which a society rests. This was also true of the new knowledge concerning the structure and dynamics of the Solar System contained in the books of Copernicus, Galileo, Kepler and at least in the developed world, has been its inability to assimilate the findings of science into its cosmology. This is the role of Astrosophy, to integrate the findings of space science into an acceptable philosophic framework. In effect we can say that if the new knowledge be compared with new wine, then philosophy must supply the new wine skins which can safely contain that wine. This has not been done for over four hundred years and the result is a dangerous fragmentation of the ideas, feelings and values that make up the totality of the psychological outlook of our society.

As regards ancient wisdom, the old and tarnished lamp of the philosophers, this is also becoming more and more inaccessible owing to a steady decline in the level of scholarship amongst the ordained priesthood. It is doubtful whether there is more than a handful of bishops living today (still less curates), who could give a convincing interpretation of either the book of Daniel or the Revelation of St. John. This is not, as one might imagine, because these books are totally inaccessible but because one of the chief keys for unlocking their mysteries is a sound knowledge of Astrology. Anyone without knowledge of the basics of Ptolemaic Astrology is unlikely to understand the framework of either Revelations or some of the other books that make up the bible. This contempt for ancient wisdom is exemplified by the way that newer churches are not orientated towards the rising Sun. This seemingly trivial detail makes a nonsense of much church symbolism and ceremonial underlining its current lack of wisdom concerning teachings old as well as new.

To counterbalance the trend, on the one hand towards secularism and on the other towards dogma, we need to dig deeper into the fabric of our culture and examine some of its roots. There is so very much that we take for granted or leave to the care of 'experts', for it often seems that we have not the time to do anything else. Perhaps it is fitting then that we should begin by examining time and how time itself fits into our cultural identity. This may give us some important clues as to what is missing in twentieth century culture.

The interpretation of time and its relationship to the processes of life has always been a deep psychological need for human beings. It is not enough to interpret time as the mere ticking of a clock, even an accurate digital watch. Time has qualities other than magnitude, for an hour at midnight is not the same as an hour at midday. We are born into a culture where the accurate measurement of the passage of time has been brought to perfection but where time itself has never seemed more meaningless. Athletic records are broken by hundredths of a second and dental appointments are logged into diaries but what note do we take of time itself? Time and space are the co-ordinates of our lives. A good farmer knows his land and also has an understanding of time and seasons, yet just as an acre of farmland differs from an acre of desert, so too does one hour from another.

Living on Earth there is only one clock that really matters and all others are made in its image. This clock is the rotating heavens from which all of life takes its time. All living things are affected profoundly by this clock in a way that they are not by the watch on a businessman's wrist. Wise men, having understood this, have in the past devised clocks in the form of sacred buildings that were also cosmic symbols. There are three cycles of time that matter beyond all others. The first of these is the day measured by the rotation of the Earth, the second is the year measured by the passage of the Sun through the zodiac and the third is the month measured by the waxing and waning of the Moon. Our calendar is based, at least vaguely, on these three cycles. However, we miss the profundity of this calendar when we show no appreciation of the 'quality' of time. Just as there are activities, such as sowing and harvesting, which can only be done properly at one given time, so also there are cycles for thought and feeling.

There has been much controversy in recent years as to whether the neolithic peoples, whom we believe to have been the builders of Stonehenge and other suchlike monuments, were capable of making the precise astronomical measurements necessary to make accurate predictions of such events as lunar eclipses. What is clear is that these structures were temples of some sort and did have some Astrosophical significance. We know from the study of Egyptian temples such as the great temple of Amon at Karnac, that these were designed in such a way that the innermost sanctuary would be illuminated by the Sun on only one day of the year. This day was when the Sun rose alongside one particular star, usually Sirius. Sir Norman Lockyer, the great Egyptologist and author of the book 'The Dawn of Astronomy' (written at the turn of the century), calculated that the Egyptians were able to measure the length of the year to within one minute by the use of a temple with an aisle 500 yards long. Such accuracy was typical of this highly developed and precise peoples. Their purpose in measuring the solstice so accurately would have stemmed from their religious customs which needed to be in exact harmony with the actual seasons. Measuring the true duration of the year would have been a bonus to knowing exactly where they were in that cycle.

As most people know, Stonehenge too is still orientated towards the point where the Sun rises on midsummer's day and the moment of sunrise is celebrated there annually by the modern Order of Druids. What is not so well known is that in mediaeval times it was traditional to build a new church with its main axis pointing from west to east, towards the point of rising of the Sun on the day of the saint to which the church was dedicated. This was a direct inheritance from the ancient wisdom of Egypt, Israel, Greece and Rome.

The cosmic connection did not end there. The church, still more the cathedral, had to fulfil multiple functions. Not only was it to be a place of worship, an enclosed space for people to gather and partake in services, but it also had to symbolise the harmony of the cycle of life. Nearly all churches are built in the shape of a cross, which is a powerful image filled with deep psychological meaning. Taken simply as the central symbol of the Christian faith, it represents the crucifixion, the figure of Christ laid out on the cross. The long nave represents the legs and trunk, the north and south transepts the arms, the choir the neck and the apse the head. In this sense the structure of the church represents the supreme symbol of the reconciliation between God and man, a permanent reminder that the necessary blood sacrifice has been made.

There is, however, another symbolism implied - one which corresponds with the movements of the Earth. If a church be orientated due east, then it follows that the Sun shines through the great east window in the early morning after sunrise. This symbolises birth and resurrection. By midday the Sun is at its zenith and has moved around to the south. Here it illuminates the church with maximum intensity symbolising the power of light, or consciousness, the victory of order over dark chaos. In most cathedrals that were originally run by monks, the cloisters and other secular buildings were placed on the south side of the church, the appropriate location for daily work. From late afternoon to dusk the Sun illuminates the west window of the church, which in French cathedrals especially is traditionally a large rose window. This time of day when work is done is the true time for meditation, quiet contemplation and prayer after the activity of the day. The rose window, lit up as a sparkling mandala by the setting Sun, has associations with the feminine aspect of life which in the Christian tradition is associated with the intervention of the Virgin Mary. At midnight the Sun passes round the north face of the church. In this quarter it is unseen as it is below the horizon. It is nighttime, the time of sleep for the body and dreams for the psyche. If south symbolises consciousness and work in the world, then north represents 'life' in the unseen world, the domain of spirits, angels and fairies.

Old church buildings convey the sense that life itself is patterned after the cycle of the day. Birth is like the morning, a time of clarity, of youth or unused potentials. The middle of life is like midday, a time when a man must take on some responsibility for the running of the world and, like St. Michael the archangel of the Sun, grapple with the forces of disorder and chaos. The time of retirement in the latter part of life is for wisdom, the mellowing of experience and a turning inwards. This then leads to death, the gateway to unseen worlds, the crossing into the realms of mind and psyche where physical bodies cannot go. This is the descent into Hades before rebirth with the Sun for another cycle of life.

Thus is enacted in the Sun's journey each day and night, as it passes through the four quarters, a symbolic play about life. Yet every circle has its centre and all rotation takes place about a pivoting axis. Where the nave, choir and transepts meet lies the mystical heart of the building. This is the still point, neither north, south, east nor west. It represents the spirit that is not seen yet, like the empty axle at the centre of a wheel, is the point of origin for all that manifests. Near this point is usually placed the eagle lectern to represent the power of the Logos, the authority of the divine. Over this crossing point is normally built the spire, a lofty structure that 'aspires' to heaven. In a symbolic way the Sun is seen to circle this pivot as it makes its daily journey through the heavens. At St. Paul's cathedral in London the great dome, which itself symbolises the heavenly sphere, is topped by a large golden cross. This cross is 365 feet above ground level and it is clear that each foot in height stands for one day of the year. In this way the architect, Sir Christopher Wren, was able to symbolise how the central axis of his church represents the axis of time, the pivot of the annual cycle.

Though the present St. Paul's is of relatively modern construction, the relationship between church buildings and the keeping of accurate time goes back to the earliest foundations. Probably the first steeples were used, amongst other things, as a crude form of gnomon, roughly indicating the hours by their lengthening shadows. Mechanical clocks did not make their appearance before about A.D. 1300 and even then they were not terribly accurate. They had to be regularly corrected either by checking with a sundial or by making careful observations of the stars. Early clocks were placed high in the church tower where they could be seen for miles around and as each hour passed, so the bells would be tolled. In fact the English word clock is derived from the French cloche meaning a bell. Larger and richer foundations, such as Salisbury or Wells cathedrals, had much more elaborate clocks that would not only display the time of day but would also indicate the position of the Sun and Moon within the astrological zodiac.

The relationship between the church and time is not confined to buildings alone. The entire structure of the Roman Catholic liturgy, that is its forms of public worship, is based upon time and the natural cycles of day, month and year. In the old monastic tradition certain hours of the day were set aside for communal prayer. These were Lauds - dawn, Prime - 6 a.m., Terce - 9 a.m., Sext - Noon, None - 3 p.m., Vespers (literally when Venus, the evening star appeared) - 5 p.m., Compline - prayers before bed, and Matins - prayers at midnight. Thus the waking day was punctuated by seven periods of prayer and for the eighth the monks would have to get up in the middle of the night.

A simpler and still commonly followed practice in Catholic countries is the reciting of the Angelus prayers. It is the custom that when the Angelus bell sounds, all other activities should cease and the people join together to recite special prayers, which are directed towards the Virgin Mary. These days the Angelus bell is normally only rung at midday but it also used to be rung at sunrise and sunset too, thus marking the three corners of the working day. The prayers of the Angelus concern the episode in the gospels when an angel appears to Mary and tells her that she is to give birth to the Messiah, even though she is still a virgin. Leaving aside any doctrinal arguments concerning parthenogenesis, it can be seen that these prayers are a reminder to look beyond the physical world and its laws and to think about that which is beyond time, the world of angels, spirits and miracles.

The liturgy of the church is not of course restricted to the daily cycle. Of probably greater significance to churchgoers is the Christian calendar of feasts, the cycle of Saints' days and Holy days. This calendar, whatever its antecedents, has a loose but explicit connection with Astrology. The church fathers who over a period of time put together the cycle of feasts, were well aware of the need to separate and celebrate the different seasons, the lunar cycle and the endless round of the year.

The ecclesiastical calendar is really composed of two interlocking cycles of feasts. The first is a solar based year that runs from Christmas to Christmas and the second is a lunar year that runs from Easter to Easter. It is in fact a very sophisticated arrangement, though the subtleties of the calendar are seldom appreciated even by the priesthood. With the decline of religious life that has taken place over the past few hundred years, many of the feasts have fallen into abeyance. Those that remain and are celebrated vigorously tend to be exploited for commercial gain. Indeed it is now difficult to separate Christmas from shopping days and Easter from chocolate. It is true that these feasts have always been times of great merriment and rejoicing but, by becoming isolated events in the religious year, they have lost much of their power and significance. There cannot be many people who are willing to make serious sacrifices for lent, the forty days leading up to Easter, still less to accept penances during advent, the four weeks prior to Christmas. However, a banquet after a fast is clearly going to have greater meaning than a continuous orgy of turkey, heavy puddings and spirits for weeks before and after the feast itself.

It is a curious paradox that we celebrate Christmas, the greatest solar festival of the year, at the time of the winter solstice, when solar power is at its weakest and the nights at their longest. The symbol of Christ as a newborn baby is closely associated with the birth of a new year, the start of a new solar cycle. From this time until midsummer the solar power continues to grow. From the time of the summer solstice it begins its long and steady decline till the following Christmas is reached.

The great lunar festival of Easter is celebrated on the

first Sunday after the first full Moon after the spring equinox. This is the time when the balance has shifted in favour of light over dark, the time when the days are at last longer than the nights again. There is a profound symbolism in the structure of the calendar. The feast of Christmas is not only the birthday of Christ but the birth of light, the son of the Sun. Easter, paradoxically, is symbolically the time of death and rebirth, the time when Christ, the son of light, has first to be sacrificed that he may then rise from the dead. It is also a time of hatching eggs. The light or life, which was born in a stable and hidden in the womb of darkness must, like a bird, come forth from the shell. The Easter egg, as many readers will doubtless know, is also a symbol of great psychological importance but the way it is represented today is only half of the whole. The original gnostic egg, from which our Easter egg is derived, has a serpent coiled around it and in this context it is worth remembering that snakes are notorious for stealing birds eggs! The serpent curled around the world-egg was an old gnostic symbol for the primordial creation and indeed the 'world girdling' serpent is a common theme of all ancient cosmologies. In later Christian symbolism it represents the 'spread of sin', for the serpent is identified with Satan, the fallen angel of wisdom, who holds the world-egg in his grip.

Whilst it is easy to understand the Easter egg as a fertility symbol, its darker meaning has been a more closely guarded secret. However, the study of Astrology provides some interesting clues concerning the inner mystery of Easter, for in Astrological symbolism, the circuit of the Moon around the Earth is stylised as a serpent or dragon. The Moon's orbit crosses the ecliptic (the path of the Sun through the sky) at two points. The dragon's head is the point where the Moon's path crosses from south to north and the opposite point, the dragon's tail, is where it crosses from north to south. These two points are not stationary but slide around the ecliptic because the relationship of the Moon's orbit to the Sun's is constantly changing. In fact they take roughly nineteen years to make one complete revolution of the ecliptic, a period of time that is referred to as the Metonic cycle. Should the Moon stand at either the dragon's head or tail when the Sun is at the same degree of the ecliptic, then a solar eclipse will take place. If they stand one at the head and the other at the tail, then there will be a lunar eclipse.

In the biblical story of the crucifixion, it is said that at the time Jesus died the sky was darkened. Since the crucifixion took place around the time of the Jewish feast of the Passover, i.e. at around the full Moon, it would have been impossible for a solar eclipse to have actually taken place. The Sun can only be eclipsed at the new Moon. Even so it seems that a 'symbolic' eclipse is being hinted at in the text, i.e. that the Moon has temporarily eaten the Sun. The Moon in this sense is likened to Satan, the dark dragon that binds the Earth and casts a spell over mankind. The secret of Easter would seem to lie in the teaching of the way of sacrifice as a means for achieving liberation from the dominion of the dragon, that is the psychic power of the Moon.

Easter and Christmas are not the only two feasts of the year that are important liturgically. In fact the year is carefully divided up by the various feast days. The seasons are separated by the four "quarter" days which are:

1) March 25th. - The feast of the annunciation to the Virgin Mary. (Lady day, after the spring equinox).

2) June 25th. - The feast of the nativity of St. John the Baptist. (Midsummers day, after the summer solstice).

3) September 29th. - The feast of St. Michael the archangel. (Michaelmas day, one week after the autumn equinox).

4) December 25th. - The Nativity of Jesus. (Christmas day, after the winter solstice).

These quarter days are all intended to be important feasts, though with the exception of Christmas they mostly pass unnoticed these days. However, if one examines them more closely, the Astrosophical meaning of these feasts is not hard to find.

The Druidical rites for the midsummer sunrise at

Stonehenge and the Scandinavian summer 'maypole' are continuations of older, pagan customs that were once widely celebrated throughout Europe. The festival of midsummer was Christianised by the church and during the middle ages it became customary to mark the occasion with a 'St. John's bonfire'. St. John the Baptist is considered by the church to have been the last of the great Hebrew prophets. He represents the summit therefore of the Old Testament revelation, just as midsummer is the peak of the previous cycle of light. To the church, St. John's birthday represents both the culmination and the death-knell of the Hebrew evangel. It is therefore both a time of merriment and of warning that the summer days are now to grow shorter, for autumn will soon approach.

The feast of Michaelmas heralds the last quarter of the year and is an invocation for spiritual protection during what is considered by many sensitives to be the most psychically active period of the year. St. Michael, who is said to be the protective archangel of the church, was also held to be responsible for the safe conduct of souls through the underworld before they faced judgement. This connection between death, the underworld, heaven and the season of autumn is echoed further with the feast of All Saints (November 1st.) and All Souls (November 2nd.). Conversely, All Hallows' E'en, which is the eve of 'All Hallows' or All Saint's, emphasises the dark aspect of autumn when witches are abroad. It was for protection against such dangers as witches spells that St. Michael's protection is invoked at Michaelmas. Until recently it was customary to have goose on the table for Michaelmas, just as we now eat turkey for Christmas. Michaelmas daisies are also so named because they flower at this time of year.

Not much more need be said about Christmas except that Santa Claus, or St. Nicholas, is really only a Christianisation of the old pagan god Odin or Woden. He was identified with the Roman god Saturn and the Greek Chronos and all of them were gods of time. Today we only think of Santa Claus as bringing presents to children but in the older mythologies the god of time brought both hope and judgement. He was connected with the concept of 'karma', which in western terms is expressed as reaping what you sow. In olden days Santa would only bring presents for children who had been good during the previous year, those who were naughty would find their stockings filled with coal. It is significant that now the gifts have become one sided, for without the threat of punishment, the image of Santa Claus as a god of Karma has lost all of its force.

Lady day, or the feast of the Annunciation, is very largely eclipsed by the greater feast of Easter that occurs at much the same time. However, the traditional, white, Easter, lilies don't really belong to that feast at all. They are properly the symbol for Lady day and also the feast of the angel Gabriel that occurs one day earlier on March 24th. The white lily represents purity, it is the flower of maidenhood, the adolescence of life. In the gospel story, it is the angel Gabriel who appears to Mary and tells her she is to conceive the child Jesus. Whether or not one believes in the possibility of a divine birth through a virgin mother, there is still the symbolic message of the Annunciation, the conjunction of spirit and matter, the marriage between Heaven and Earth. The flowers of spring, which are all 'virgins' until pollinated by the insects, represent the possibility and fertility of life. Living beings are able to perpetuate their species through the power of sex, which is not operational until puberty. The white lily represents fecundity, a flower which is open and therefore, like the sexual organs of a teenage girl, able to be fertilised for the first time. The sexuality of spring has been sublimated in church symbolism, the emphasis being put upon virginity rather than promiscuity but the underlying theme of springtime eros cannot be escaped entirely. It goes without saying that the earlier, pagan rites of spring were never so prudish.

A deeper study of church symbolism, ritual and doctrine would go beyond the scope of this book and probably bore most readers. Surfice it to say that Astrosophical ideas have been at the very heart of Christianity for nearly two thousand years and the decline of the church has been parallelled by a gradual diminishment in its acceptance of the importance of cosmology as a part of its teaching. Perhaps if more attention were paid to the treasury of symbolism and tradition employed by the mediaeval church the slide could be halted and more people be attracted by what it has to offer. What is clear is that every religion has the duty to provide its followers with a sound cosmology, if this duty is abdicated then the priesthood have only themselves to blame if people turn to atheistic science for a convincing explanation of their origins.

CHAPTER 3

The Art of Measure

Whilst we cannot say very much about how early man perceived the natural world, it is clear that since the dawn of the neolithic era at least, time as well as space has been an overriding concern of the human race. These two, time and space, make up the fundamental framework of the physical universe and the accurate measurement of both has always been regarded as of the highest importance.

The British Imperial system of measures is of extreme antiquity. At first sight the units of spatial measure in this system, that is to say inches, feet, yards, chains, furlongs etc. seem arbitrary and the system needlessly complex. Why not do away with it completely and go over to the metric system? Why continue with an old fashioned system at all? The voices for change have been loud this century, for the commercial and economic pressures for a simplified system have outweighed the philosophical and metaphysical arguments for keeping our older, more sophisticated and complex system.

One reason for keeping the old system of measure is that it is based upon profound insights as to the relationship between measure, pattern and time. What appear to be quite arbitrary divisions of units are actually used to enable the exact relationship between length and area to be defined. The system is also able to accommodate circular measures and thus to equate squares with circles (the famous squaring of the circle) without recourse to fractions or the need to evaluate pi. This can most easily be seen in the relationship of the yard to the chain. Because 22 yards makes up one chain, it naturally follows that the perimeter of a circle with diameter of 14 yards is 44 yards, or two chains. This is derived from the mathematical formula:

Circumference = pi x Diameter.
Therefore: C = pi x 14
= 22/7 x 14
= 22 x 2
= 44 yards
= 2 chains

Thus a circle of radius seven yards will automatically have a perimeter of 2 chains. It follows from this that a circle with a radius of 35 yards will have a perimeter of 220 yards = 10 chains = 1 furlong.

This brings us to the very useful relationship between the yard and the inch. Because there are 36 inches to the yard, it naturally follows that there are 360 inches to 10 yards. This relationship readily lends itself to splitting up the circle into arcs of exact length. Since there are 360 degrees to a circle, each degree corresponds with 1 360 of the circumference. For a circle with a perimeter of 1 furlong, each degree of angle at the centre corresponds to 220/360 yards = 22 inches.

Thus it can be seen that this system of proportional units makes it very easy to equate length with angles and arcs of circumference and indeed it has been used since time immemorial for just this purpose. The totality of the system was known as the 'Canon of Measure' and knowledge of it was considered to be a sacred trust, for it had to be preserved from corruption.

One of the main aims of the ancient canon of measure was to find and interpret the natural relationships between space, time and matter. In every culture worthy of the name, the exact standardisation of measure has been of prime concern. The principle standard that is needed is length. Once a unit of length has been established, then other units of area, volume and weight can be derived from it. For the Ancient Egyptians, whose system of weights and measures we have largely inherited (though in a disguised form), the primal unit of measure was the cubit. Different length of cubit were used at different times and in different places for reasons that will be discussed later, but what concerns us here is the standard Egyptian Geographic Cubit and this measures one and a half feet.

Royal Cubit 21 inches
Cubit 18 inches
Foot 12 inches
Hand 3 inches

To calculate the height of a horse we still make use of another ancient unit, the hand. This unit, in Egyptian times, measured 4 fingers. That is to say the width across 4 fingers excluding the thumb. The inch was an ancient measure, reckoned to be the length of the top joint of the thumb. 1 foot was measured as equal to 16 fingers, which in turn was equal to 4 hands or 12 inches. Thus 1 hand was equal to 3 inches. (N.B.. Today's equestrians use a 'Hand' of 4 inches instead of the 4 fingers it should be, this means there are now only 3 hands to the foot instead of 4.)

Using the ancient value of the hand as 4 fingers, there are 6 hands to an ordinary, geographic cubit of oneand a half feet and 7 hands to a longer unit known as a Royal Cubit. The Ancient Egyptians used both cubits, the latter being especially useful where it was necessary to divide lengths by 7.

Standard units of volume are also extremely important and can be arrived at by cubing a standard length to obtain a standard cubic capacity. Using the Egyptian geographic cubit, we can obtain the length of a foot of $^2/_3$ cubits. The cube of this foot gives the fundamental Egyptian measure of volume, the Artaba and this unit was used throughout the ancient world. The Artaba itself could be subdivided into 64 pints, which would each be cubes of side 4 fingers or 3 inches.

To obtain standard units of weight in the ancient world, special measuring cylinders were made and these were precisely calibrated to hold an exact volume of water. For most practical purposes this was considered to be accurate enough and metallic weights were fashioned to equal exactly the weight of this volume of water. The chief standard of weight for measuring gold was the Qedet and the weight of 1 Egyptian pint of water was equal to 50 qedets. A much larger unit of weight was the Talent. This was derived from the Roman as opposed to Egyptian foot and was equal to 2880 qedets. It was generally reckoned that a man, equipped with a yoke and collar, could carry a maximum weight of 2 talents. It was therefore a very useful unit of measure in the days when most carrying was done by slave power!

There are very many other units of measurement that derive from the few discussed here and indeed weights and measures are a fascinating study in themselves. However, as the subject has been covered exhaustively in the appendix by Prof. L.C.Stecchini to Peter Tompkins book *The Secrets of the Great Pyramid*, no-more need be said here. The important point to remember about ancient systems of measure is that the units are all derived in the first place from a single unit of linear measure called the cubit. As we shall see, this was itself derived in a most remarkable way from the study of Astronomy.

We must remember that the Earth is a spinning sphere and that because of this the Sun rises and sets. At any given moment it is dark on one side of the planet and light upon the other. In one place it is sunrise and in another sunset. Every point on the planetary sphere has its own unique local time, which in turn is related directly to the movement of the Sun. At noon local time at any point in the northern hemisphere, the Sun will always be at its maximum elongation for the day and it will always be exactly due south. However, if it is noon in London, then further west in Bristol it is still a few minutes before 12 using local time. This discrepancy goes unnoticed by us because we have adopted a standard time for the whole of Britain based upon Greenwich Mean Time. True time, however, will always lag behind GMT for points further west and be ahead for those further east.

To see how this affects the canon of measure, we must first give some consideration to the way that we measure time. Our clock of hours, minutes and seconds is perhaps the most enduring legacy we have of the ancient Mesopotamian civilisation better known as Babylon. Whereas the Egyptians were brilliant geometers, the Sumerians and their later descendants the Babylonians were experts at arithmetic. Their methods of counting were, however, very different from our own. In addition to using a decimal system similar to today's, they also used a 'hexagessimal' system. This system, as the name would suggest, involved counting in sixties. This sounds extremely complicated, but for certain purposes it is very useful as 60 can be divided into many whole-number factors. Their main reason for adopting this system was their fascination with Astrology. Counting in 60's gives a simple correspondence with the observed movement of the Sun.

We know very well that there are 365 1/4 days to the solar year. As this is an awkward number to work with, the solar calendar was rounded to 360 days plus 5 extra intercalary days between years. Since the year corresponds to an entire cycle, it was useful to divide up the circle into 360 degrees. Thus the Sun is seen to progress through the zodiac by almost exactly 1 degrees per day. As 360 is divisible by 60, it is probable that this natural division of the year gave the inspiration to the Babylonians to adopt a hexagessimal system of arithmetic.

In the west, for reasons of history and practicality in other matters, we have blended the Babylonian system of counting in sixties with the Egyptian way of splitting the day into hours. In their system day and night were each split into 12 hours, giving 24 hours in all. Given a clear sky, the time of day could be measured with sundials during daylight hours and from the movement of the stars at night. In one hour of time the Earth has rotated on its axis by 360/24 = 15 degrees of arc. If it is 12 noon local time at one place, then it is only 11 a.m. at another which is 15 degrees of longitude further west and already 1 p.m. at place 15 degrees east. Thus it appears to us as though the Sun is moving westwards with an angular velocity of 15 degrees per hour. From this measured rotational velocity we can calculate actual measurements of distance and it was on these measurements that the ancient Egyptians, and probably other civilised peoples, based their systems of measure.

Nearer to home local time at Bristol, for example, lags Greenwich Mean Time by 10 minutes. From this we can calculate that Bristol lies $2 \frac{1}{2}$ degrees west of the Greenwich meridian. If we could measure the geographical distance between Bristol and Greenwich, then we could work out a relationship between distance and rotational velocity of the Earth. We could calculate what length corresponds with one degree of longitude at the latitude of Bristol and London. From this we could develop a standard unit of length which, as it is based on the spin of the Earth, would be astronomically meaningful. This unit would integrate all of our other units of measure for it would directly relate our experience of space with time.

As has been said earlier, the Ancient Egyptians were

extremely good geometers and one of their prime concerns was to establish the correctness of their system of weights and measures. Central to Egyptian religion and philosophy was the concept of 'Maat', a word which can be translated as truth, legality. It was believed by the Egyptians that after a person died his or her soul would leave the body and be taken to the hall of judgement. Here the symbolic Canopic jar containing the heart of the deceased would be weighed in the balances against the feather of truth, Maat. If the result were favourable, then the soul could proceed to the Egyptian heaven, if not then it would be eaten by a monster which was part lion and part crocodile. The symbol of the heart being balanced against a feather implies that what is being weighed is not the physical heart but rather its spiritual content. The feather of Maat, which would itself float in the breeze, represents the abstract, spiritual quality of truth.

We can see from this in what high regard the Egyptians, who were not primitive people, held the law, Maat. To arrive at a system of measures that was in accordance with cosmic truth was therefore given a very high priority. In order to do this, they standardised their geographical cubit by reference to the spin of the Earth at the equator. They calibrated the geographical cubit in such a way that the equatorial rotational velocity of the Earth is 1000 geographic cubits per second.

As we have already seen, having once arrived at a standard of measure for length, the cubit, they were then able to derive all other measures from this. By basing their system of measures upon the rate of rotation of the Earth (actually measured by observing the movements of stars), they were able to create a link between daily life and the greater, cosmic creation. The result of such careful attention to detail was to bring into their culture a consciousness of pattern, harmony, mathematics and aesthetics. From this foundation arose the remarkable achievements of their architecture and a civilisation which was able to endure for thousands of years.

It is this legacy, albeit modified over the centuries, which has come down to us today as the British Imperial system of measures. As to whether it will last beyond the end of this century is debatable, for it is the expressed wish of government to sweep aside tradition and to replace feet, yards, gallons, pints, tons and ounces with the 'atheistic' metric system of metres, kilograms and litres. If they are successful in this then one more symbolic link between man and cosmos will have been broken and our culture will be that much the poorer.

CHAPTER 4

Astrology and Divination.

Astrosophical wisdom has found expression in many surprising ways, one of these is the game of Roulette and another is the ordinary pack of playing cards. Gambling is, in a sense, only a form of applied divination. It is therefore not surprising to find that the most commonly played games of chance are based on traditional systems of divination.

The Roulette wheel is a direct descendant of the mediaeval wheel of fortune, the traditional symbol for the inevitability of fate. It is not hard to see the connection between the wheel of fortune and that other great, symbolic 'wheel' in the sky, the zodiac. There are twelve signs of the zodiac and each of these is composed of three decanates, making thirty six in all. If we add the number zero, which symbolises the point of balance at the centre of the wheel, then we can see that this gives us the basis for the Roulette wheel.

It is quite probable that the Roulette wheel was originally used as a method of divination, an oracle. The chance landing of the ball into one of the slots can easily be given astrological or numerological interpretation in accordance with accepted practice. Each decanate of a sign is traditionally assigned to one of the planetary rulers of the elementary triplicity to which that sign belongs. This may sound difficult but it isn't really. A triplicity is simply a family of three signs that belong to the same element (for example Aries, Leo and Sagittarius make up the fire triplicity).Thus the number 1 would correspond with the first decanate of Aries, which is the period of the first ten days of spring and the first decan of Aries is ruled by Mars (ruler of Aries), the second by the Sun (ruler of Leo) and the third by Jupiter (ruler of Sagittarius). The number 1 can therefore be interpreted as, the first ten days of spring, emergence from hibernation, the beginning or resurrection of some matter, or to the beginning of some bold or rash enterprise.

Using a table of decanates and a certain amount of intuition, the Roulette wheel could be used again as an effective form of divination and the result would be a system somewhat similar to the Chinese *I Ching* (Book of Changes) but with its roots in western mysticism rather than eastern. The number zero would be like the joker in a pack of cards and would imply that the matter on hand was unpredictable, for the unexpected is a factor that operates in the real world and learning to deal with unforeseen circumstances is part of the skill of life. Here is an attempt at such a table.

To use the Roulette wheel as a method of divination, it is first necessary to frame a question. A simple "yes" or "no" answer could be determined by if the ball landed on a red or black number. If there is a question relating to time, then the period of the year indicated by the number and its associated decanate should also be considered. To answer questions related to other matters, then a system of correspondence is needed (such as the keyword chart printed here). Clearly, for the oracle to be effective, then there needs to be a fair degree of intuition at play as well. The keywords should be used as just that, keys which jog the mind and bring the answer to consciousness.

Roulette of course is mainly a game of chance and this begs the question as to where chance ends and fate begins. The Jungian theory of synchronicity is an attempt to explain coincidence without resort to a system of cause and effect. An example of its working is when you think of someone only to find a letter from them in your letter box or to have a phone call from them later that day. Jung called this sort of happening synchronicity, the way that similar events tend to cluster together in daily life.

By applying the Jungian theory of synchronicity to

Roulette, it should be possible to discover what are the lucky numbers at any given time. Because the Roulette wheel is a model of the rotating zodiac, so there should be a synchronous link between the numbers that come up and the pattern of the heavens above. If this is so, then a lucky number should be one that corresponds with a lucky decanate. If we were going to use this as a basis for gambling, then worthwhile choices would be:

a)   The decan at the midheaven position.

b)   The decan occupied by Jupiter.

c)   The decan occupied by the "Pars Fortunae" or Moon's north node.

More complicated systems of Astrology would no doubt reveal other lucky numbers but it is difficult to draw a distinct line between thoughtful predictions based on synchronicity and superstition. The whole point about Roulette is that it is a game of chance and absolutely nothing can be predicted with any certainty. There are always unknown factors and hazard is an ever present condition throughout creation. Wise people leave gambling to those with more time and money than sense.

If few people have a Roulette wheel in their home, then probably most have a pack of playing cards. Like roulette these are said to have originated in France. Our ordinary pack of 52 cards is derived from the older pack of 56 cards that make up the Minor Arcana of the tarot. The joker meanwhile is not a later addition but a carry over of the unnumbered tarot "fool" card that acts as a link between the 56 cards of the minor arcana and the 21 trumps that make up the major.

The ordinary pack of cards is one of the most sophisticated systems of astrological divination ever conceived. The tarot itself, though it has many borrowings from earlier philosophical and religious thought, is essentially a system of Christian mysticism. The earliest tarot pack known is the Marseilles and this would suggest that the original formulators of the tarot were members of a secret

Christian sect existing in the Mediterranean area. At first sight the Cathars of southern France might seem logical candidates, however their doctrines, in as far as we know them, seem quite at odds with tarot symbolism. It seems much more likely that the tarot was first developed in Alexandria and then brought to France by "gypsies", i.e. Egyptians. This would explain the strong gnostic element that can be seen in the tarot symbols.

In the ordinary pack of playing cards, the 52 cards represent the 52 weeks of the year, the joker representing the extra day (2 days in a leap year) that make up the full compliment of 365(6) days. The four suits represent the four seasons, (though there is much disagreement amongst cartomancers as to which suit corresponds with which season). If we go back to the original suits of the tarot, from which our playing cards are derived, they can give us some important clues as to what was the original allocation of suits with seasons. The playing card and tarot suits correspond as follows:

Diamonds = Pentacles

Hearts   = Cups

Spades   = Swords

Clubs   = Wands

The tarot suits are exactly the same in format as the ordinary playing cards with the exception that they have four additional court cards called 'knights'. The reason for this is obscure but may relate to the fact that 56 is divisible by 7 as well as four. The additional cards may also have been inserted to cover up the hidden numerology of the pack and its connections with Astrology. Curiously the modern pack of playing cards is far more explicit in this matter.

The ordinary suits of cards are divided into red and black, hearts and diamonds being red and clubs and spades black. Astrologically this would seem to indicate the split of the year into two halves. At the spring equinox the Sun passes over the ecliptic and moves into the northern hemisphere. At this time of year the days are longer than the nights, light has dominance over dark. The 26 weeks that follow the spring equinox correspond with the red cards of the pack and are considered to be positive. At the autumn equinox the Sun goes south over the ecliptic and there is a reversal as the nights grow longer and the days shorter. This period is represented by the black cards.

If we return to the minor arcana of the tarot, then it is clear that the naming of the suits relates to the celebration of the major feasts of the Christian calendar that mark the four quarters of the year. The correspondence is as follows:

1) Summer is represented by the suit of cups, the container of water,because the feast at the start of summer is the birth of John the Baptist on June 25th. In the later pack of playing cards this became the suit of hearts, the "chalice" of blood within the human body.

2) Autumn is represented by the suit of swords and it starts with Michaelmas, the feast of St. Michael the archangel and the carrier of the sword of justice. It is the time of judgement, weighing and execution.

3) Winter is represented by the sprouting wand which symbolises Christ as the fulfiller of the prophecy in Isaiah chapter 1 that a shoot would rise from the stump of Jesse. The 'stump of Jesse' is the house of King David, the 'tree' having been hacked down by the Babylonians at the time of King Zedekiah. Jesus is said to have descended from this line at the start of the Gospels. The mystery of Christmas is one of rebirth, a fresh start both for the tree of Jesse in the manger of Bethlehem, the city of David, and the rebirth of the power of light.

4) Diamonds, or pentacles, represent the time of spring. This is because of the association of the pentagram with the mystery of the Virgin Mary whose principal feast, the Annunciation, begins the spring quarter. It is the time especially associated with the

regeneration of life from the womb of the Earth and the pentagram is a symbol derived from nature and the laws of growth. The number five is witnessed in the five petals of the wild dog-rose and in the five decades of the catholic rosary, both of which are closely associated with the veneration of the Virgin. In church mysticism the number 5 is also allied with the other great feast of spring, Easter. This is because of the five wounds inflicted on Christ during the Crucifixion. These five wounds are today symbolised at Easter by the five nails which are pushed into the Paschal candle, which is lit on Easter Sunday and at all the services throughout Paschal-tide, the period of forty days between Easter and Ascension day. The candle symbolises the risen Christ as the light of the world and the five nails his wounds.

By association with the events of Easter, Pentacles are associated with sacrifice and therefore the need for charity. In some tarot packs they are called coins and represent not just wealth but also generosity and the giving of alms. This

Table of Court cards to Month/sign		
Card	*Month*	*Sign*
King of Clubs	January	Capricorn
Queen of Clubs	February	Aquarius
Knave of Clubs	March	Pisces
King of Diamonds	April	Aries
Queen of Diamonds	May	Taurus
Knave of Diamonds	June	Gemini
King of Hearts	July	Cancer
Queen of Hearts	August	Leo
Knave of Hearts	September	Virgo
King of Spades	October	Libra
Queen of Spades	November	Scorpio
Knave of Spades	December	Sagittarius

is still symbolised in Britain where the sovereign hands out Maundy money to certain old age pensioners on Maundy Thursday. This again takes place just before Easter.

The division of the playing cards into two types, the ordinary numbered cards and the court cards, enables other useful correspondences to be found. The court cards can be said to each represent one of the months of the year or signs of the zodiac. This gives rise to the following table of correspondences:

The four suits of cards are also considered to represent the fourfold division of Man. These divisions are body, soul, mind and spirit and they correspond to diamonds, hearts, spades and clubs respectively.

The numbered cards are closely related to the ideas of Christian Kabbalah, (a borrowing from the hidden teachings of Judaism). The numbers from one to ten, repeated for the four suits, represent the ten Sephiroth, or 'emanations', as they manifest on four different planes of existence (roughly corresponding with the four levels of man). The numbered cards can also be treated as an abbreviated pack of forty cards. In this case each card is considered to represent one day, the whole pack containing a micro year of forty days. This period is not as artificial as it sounds, for forty days is $1/9$ of 360 and therefore symbolic of $1/9$ of a circle and $1/9$ of a year. In the church calendar there are three important periods of 40 days each: Lent (the period from Ash Wednesday to Easter), Paschaltide (the period from Easter to Ascension day) and Christmastide (the period from Christmas to Candlemas, the feast of the purification of the Virgin).

It is one of the remarkable and fortuitous accidents of history that playing cards should have become so popular and therefore widespread. The pack of cards is rightly called the 'poor man's bible', for it contains in essence form the teachings of Christian Astrology and kabbalah and points the way towards an understanding of cosmic rhythm. The cards are a genuine work of art for they form a bridge between Heaven and Earth and provide a set of keys with which many mysteries may be unlocked. That they have also become the principle means through which man is able to indulge in one of his worst vices, gambling, should not detract from the hidden wisdom of the cards themselves. As so often happens with noble enterprises, the bridge that may lead to heaven has a shadow, a negative counterpart that leads to hell. We can perhaps allow ourselves a wry smile when we consider that the gambling joints of the western world are custodians and preservers of the ancient wisdom. The cards themselves are neither good nor evil, they are a means and not an end. What use we make of them depends upon us ourselves.

III

Philosophy and the Stars

CHAPTER 1

A Common Language.

Thus far we have considered anew firstly the structure and dynamics of the physical universe and secondly some of the ways in which astronomical ideas, measures and time periods have influenced human culture. To say that such things as church liturgy, weights and measures and games of chance are based upon natural cycles of time and space is but to state the obvious. There are, however, other and deeper mysteries garbed in the cloaks of astronomy and astrology. It is to this hidden wisdom that we must now turn if we would have deeper insight into the mysteries of Astrosophy.

We live at a time when our culture is fragmenting. Ours is the age of the specialist, the expert and the bureaucrat. Our knowledge of the physical world has become so diversified that it is quite impossible for any one person to stay at the forefront of every discipline, for new discoveries are being made daily. Add to this the growing complexity of such important areas as the law, commerce, finance, taxation, the media, computing and engineering and it becomes clear why this has to be the age of the professional, the man who 'professes' mastery in his chosen field.

This elevation of the specialist has had two very damaging side effects on our civilisation. The first is that it has transferred status (and often wealth) to people, who though highly knowledgeable in their own area, may be totally 'undeveloped' in other ways. (We have all, for example, met the type of scientist who though brilliant at mathematics yet as a man remains sexually, emotionally and artistically immature.) The second problem arises from what may be called the 'Tower of Babel' effect. The more fragmented our culture becomes, the harder it is for the 'experts' to communicate with one another on more than the most superficial levels.

We are not here talking of the sciences themselves, for by and large scientists all speak dialects of the same language, mathematics. No, the greater problems of communication arise where divides between disciplines are greater. For example, what level of communication can there be between a barrister and a sculptor, or a physicist and a priest? Each profession has its own unique view of the world. One sees it in terms of material forces, another as shapes, a third in terms of international law and the fourth as the realm of angels, saints and spirits. The subtle insights obtained through professional study in a restricted field cannot be easily conveyed to those who are not also specialists in the same area. The common language of, say, English is inadequate for expressing inner meanings which require a high degree of intuitive insight rather than words if they are to be grasped.

Problems of communication have always existed, though it was still possible until fairly recently for men such as Leonardo da Vinci or Isaac Newton to be 'Universalists', experts in nearly all areas of important knowledge. For us lesser mortals a simpler solution has to be found and in fact this has always in the past been provided by the truly universal language of symbolism. Symbols can be divided into two types: those whose meaning is intrinsic (that is to say the interpretation of the symbol is possible through direct analysis of the symbol content itself) and those which are conventional (that is the symbol can only be understood properly if one already knows what it signifies). Astrology is mainly concerned with the use and interpretation of symbols of the first type, those whose meaning is intrinsic.

An example of an intrinsic symbol is the zodiacal sign of Scorpio. This sign occupies the middle month of the autumn quarter, the time of death and decay. Appropriately it is given the symbol of the scorpion, one of the most deadly creature on Earth. The time of the scorpion symbolises the period of the year when death walks the face of the Earth striking plants dead with the first frosts of autumn. It is also traditionally the time when excess livestock would be killed and the meat preserved in salt .

Less obvious symbols used in Astrology are the attributions of the names of various Roman gods to the planets. The planet Venus for example, which we think of as the planet of affections and love, was attributed by the Mesopotamians to the goddess Astarte, whose brief covered not only love but also war. It is important to realise that in the ancient world the names of the gods and goddesses came first and only later were these names applied to the heavenly bodies which were considered most suitable as auguries of the invisible principle named as a 'god'. The belief in planetary radiations and direct influence is a much later theory. The original Astrology of the Sumerians and Babylonians was based upon the theory of correspondence, that what was written in the stars was sure to happen upon the Earth, that the greater cosmos is mirrored in the lesser. In this schema it was appropriate to allocate particular attributes to individual heavenly bodies and then to use their movements as a method of divination. The essential element in this was always the perceptiveness of the astrologer and his ability to read what was important and ignore the rest.

The system of western Astrology that has come down to us is in reality a compendium of several different systems, the Babylonian, the Egyptian, the Greek and the mediaeval to name but a few. To understand the deeper teachings of Astrology, it is necessary to peel back the different layers and assess their individual contributions to the whole. It is then that the system becomes intelligible. The use of Astrology for making horoscopes and forecasts is really only one aspect of what in reality is a fascinating art. The basis of all practical Astrology is the theory of cosmoses. According to this theory all complete entities can be given the name cosmos, that is an organised and self-contained whole. Thus on one scale man is a cosmos, on a smaller scale a single cell is a cosmos, and on a larger scale the

Solar System is a cosmos. Thus it is said that Man is a microcosm of the macrocosm, a small entity that carries within himself the image of the greater universe, the macrocosm.

This same teaching was always the fundamental tenet of all religious, philosophical and metaphysical systems from the time of Abraham to the modern age beginning in the late 18th century. In the book of Genesis, for example, it is said that man is created in the image of God, which implies that by studying man, one is also studying the likeness of his creator. It is only during the last two hundred years that this teaching has been discarded in favour of more tangible, materialistic philosophies. Before then it was considered self-evident that Man is the measure of all things, that by studying man it is possible to understand all of creation.

In the terminology of Astrology the doctrine of cosmoses is expressed in the pithy saying: 'As above, so below'. Translated mundanely, this teaching is the fundamental philosophy behind the science of prediction and the study of auguries. However, no real astrologer or wiseman is really interested in horoscopes or in trying to predict Derby winners. Such activities as these are like playing video games on a computer, fun but trivial pursuits that should not be taken too seriously. It is very likely that in the ancient world Astrology was chiefly taught as a system of Psychology. The use of Astrology for divination would have been an outward justification for its study rather than its real purpose, just as in the middle ages the search for the Holy Grail was a justification for the study of the symbols of esoteric Christianity, the physical cup never having been the true object of the quest.

The principle symbols of Astrology are arranged into sets or groups, which if taken together give a pattern of wholeness, a description of an entire cosmos. Thus the twelve signs of the zodiac, which make up the circuit of the year, are also applicable to man himself as a microcosmos, each part of him being ascribed to a particular sign of the zodiac. Similarly the traditional seven planets (which include the Sun and Moon), form a set of distinct types or variants on a theme. We can compare them with the seven colours of the rainbow, for just as all colours are frequencies of light, so all the planets are heavenly bodies and just as the colours of the rainbow form a 'set' which if taken in its entirety is white light, so the planets form a set which we call the Solar System.

Because the principle symbols of Astrology: the zodiac and planets, are themselves archetypal forms with deep intrinsic meaning, they have been borrowed and used in many diverse ways and contexts. Just as colour symbolism is habitually invoked to describe the political complexions of people and parties, so also astrological terminology can be used to describe anything which is itself a cosmic process, whether macrocosmic or microcosmic. In the past it has found application in such diverse fields as Human Psychology, Medicine, Herbalism, Alchemy and Architecture. These are not trivial usages but a sensible and practical method of communication, for the symbols and terminology of Astrology form a natural language which can allow meaningful dialogue between specialists in different fields. In this sense Astrology is the mother of all arts and sciences, for it is able to supply them with a cosmic, archetypal language. Cultures and societies which have made use of astrological symbols have generally been well integrated. The disappearance over the last two hundred years of this sense of cosmic identity between the lesser universe of man and the greater cosmos of space has been parallelled by a more general fragmentation of our society and the feeling of alienation and cultural worthlessness so typical of our times.

It is the use of Astrology as a means of describing diverse systems and processes and of relating them to a whole that raises it above the level of idle superstition and makes it a worthwhile study. To make this clearer we need to first investigate its symbolism and then see how it has been applied to fields far removed from the night sky. It will become apparent that the study of Astrology is as much a study of man himself as it is of the universe in which he lives.

CHAPTER 2

Esoteric Astrology.

The twelve signs of the zodiac, that is to say the twelve divisions of the ecliptic, have inherited the names of the stellar constellations that at one time corresponded with the positions of the Sun in the twelve solar 'months' from one spring equinox to the next. Now, because of the precession of the equinoxes, the Sun does not actually occupy the physical constellation at the exact time of the year that one would at first expect. The Sun currently passes the spring equinox whilst it is still in the constellation of Pisces, the fish. It does not actually pass into the constellation of Aries, the ram, until about a month later. It is still customary, however, to start the zodiac with the sign of Aries as the first month of spring and to divide the year into twelve equal periods, giving them the names of signs which now bear no relation to the actual movement of the Sun amongst the stars.

This is probably the most confusing aspect of Astrology and the cause of much scepticism. It should, however, be realised that what is being measured is the year as a cycle of time with direct relationship to the Sun not the stars. The philosophy that lies behind Astrology is concerned more with time than space and in particular with cycles of time. The cycle of the Sun still goes through twelve symbolic stages regardless of the starry background and in the language of symbolism it is still correct to start with Aries at the spring equinox and to end with Pisces.

This immediately brings us to the question of why we have twelve signs and not eleven or thirteen. This is a good question and needs to be answered. Were it not that the human psyche itself is structured at the unconscious level, then probably the zodiac would have little or no relevance at all. However, there is a definite structure or pattern inherent in the unconscious and it is to appeal to this that such systems as the zodiac have been devised.

C.G. Jung in his many volumes of writings again and again stresses the importance of the mandala as a symbol of wholeness. He found as an empirical fact that the spontaneous paintings and sketches of his patients would almost always correspond with mandala symbolism. Most commonly they would draw designs based upon a circle containing a cross, or some other means of dividing it into four equal partitions. From his researches he discovered that the cross is a fundamental symbol of the psyche representing wholeness, completion and unity.

In contrast the triangle or trinity represents dynamisms. The trinity always relates to three independent forces that bear a definite relationship to one another such that one is active, one is passive and the third neutral. United and taken together they make up a fourth, which is higher than the other three and contains them. Thus red, green and blue are the three primary colours. Taken separately we can say that red is active, blue is passive and green neutral. If the three colours are blended together in equal proportions then they will give white which is a total colour and higher than the other three. On the human level we see the father principle as active, the mother as passive and the child as neutral. Taken together we have the fourth principle, the 'family' which is total and contains all the other three.

By this sort of reasoning we can see the meaning of the zodiac. There are twelve signs and twelve is the product of three and four. Four itself is a totality number. It represents the four aspects or phases of something. Thus there are four seasons, four phases of the Moon and the four cardinal points of the compass.

There are other less obvious groups of four such as birth, growth, maturity and decay; root, stem. flower and fruit; sweet, sour, bitter and salty; and solid, liquid, vapour and flame. It is this last that concerns us most in Astrology as it is used as the archetype of all cycles of four. All of the twelve signs of the zodiac are said to belong to one or another of the four basic 'elements', i.e. Fire, Earth, Air and Water. There are therefore three signs belonging to each element which, so to speak, make up the *family* of that element.

It is customary in astrology to think of man as a being living at one and the same time within four different realms. Man is a multi-faceted being who, unlike a robot, is able to live within different worlds and on different levels. The first and most obvious of these is the physical, the material world of base matter from which is drawn the physical body. Symbolically speaking we can call this level 'Earth'. The second world is one of feeling, of sensitivity, atmosphere, subtlety and mood. This level is symbolised by the element 'Water' and is sometime termed the astral plane to distinguish it from the physical. The third level is one of thought, mentality, reason and logic. This level is known as the mental plane and is symbolised by the element 'Air'. Finally there is the fourth plane, known as the spiritual, which is related to the deepest intuition and the functioning of the faculty of will. This level is symbolised by the element of fire.

To illustrate further how the symbols of the zodiac relate to man, let us take just one of these worlds, the physical, and see how the signs are related to it. Although the physical body which exists on the earth plane is only one of the levels of being, nevertheless it contains within it a mirror of the whole. We can say that the body itself contains a fiery, an airy, a watery and an earthy part. Earth corresponds to the physical structures of the body, the flesh and bones. Water is everywhere present in the river of the bloodstream and within every cell. Air also is drawn into the lungs and suffuses every part. Fire is present in the warmth of the body, the essential heat generated by internal combustion, absorbed from sunlight of from the hearthside. We can therefore divide the physical body amongst the ruling elements and the signs of the zodiac according to the following system:

1) Earth signs.

Capricorn   rules the bones.
Taurus   rules the muscles.
Virgo   rules the viscera and organs.

2) Water signs.

Cancer   rules the digestive juices and mucous
            secretions.
Scorpio   rules the generative fluids, menstruum,
            cerebro-spinal fluid and puss.
Pisces   rules the bloodstream.

3) Air signs.

Gemini   rules the breath and speech.
Libra   rules the air pockets in the head, lungs and
            intestines.
Aquarius   rules the air dissolved in the blood and
            tissues.

4) Fire signs.

Aries   rules the heat in the blood generated by
            passion, rage, anger or desire.
Leo   rules the radiated heat from the body, the
            emanation and aura of a living being.
Sagittarius rules the heat from the muscles generated
            by work, movement, sport or other activity.

From these twelve we can see that we have an entire analysis of the substance making up the human body when considered only from the earthly or physical standpoint. A more common way of dividing up the human body astrologically is to look at only what is externally visible. This system is met with in many astrological textbooks and is often represented diagrammatically with the picture of a man curled around the zodiac, his feet touching the back of his head. This system gives rise to the following table of rulerships:

Aries	rules the head.
Taurus	rules the neck.
Gemini	rules the shoulders and arms.
Cancer	rules the breast.
Leo	rules the upper back.
Virgo	rules the abdomen.
Libra	rules the lower back.
Scorpio	rules the pelvis.
Sagittarius	rules the hips and thighs.
Capricorn	rules the knees.
Aquarius	rules the lower legs and ankles.
Pisces	rules the feet.

The point behind such systems as these is not a superstitious belief in human anatomy and cosmic fate but rather to draw attention to the inner teaching that 'man is the measure of all things', that the human body is a totality which mirrors the greater totality of the cosmic zodiac.

Planetary Astrology is also based upon the 'law' of correspondences, that is to say what happens above is reflected in what happens below. Many astrologers , past and present, believe that the principle bodies of the Solar System each emanate a special, subtle 'ray'. Before the discovery of the planet Uranus, there were seven known bodies in the System in addition to the Earth. There were therefore seven rays, which neatly corresponded with the seven colours of the rainbow into which sunlight can be split. Modern astrologers, unwilling to abandon the theory of rays, have added three more, those of Uranus, Neptune and Pluto.

According to this modern system of Astrology, at each moment of day and night, there is a changing emphasis in the intensity of these rays, some 'colours' growing stronger and some weaker. The astrologer, by following the movements of the stars and planets, is able to read the horoscope (literally the picture of the hour). Some planets are thought to augment or enhance the power of others and some are thought to act in detriment to each other. He therefore has to also pay careful attention to the relative angles between the planets and consider whether they are 'conjunct', 'square', 'trine' etc. so that he can deduce their relative strengths and weaknesses.

In addition to all this data, he or she must also consider the particular positions of the planets within the signs of the zodiac, which sign is rising, which culminating and which setting. As if this weren't enough there are also systems of 'house' to contend with, for depending upon the position of the planet in relation to the horizon, so it is in one or another house. It can be seen from all of this that Genethliacal Astrology, to give it its proper name, is a highly complicated business and even then at the end of the day, so much depends upon the astrologer's ability to interpret all of this data.

In many ways the development of the system of Astrology, so that it can incorporate the more recently discovered outer planets, has been a great mistake. The theory of planetary emanations, which is scoffed at by most astronomers, is really only a cover for the deeper and more esoteric level of planetary Astrology. This in its essence is closely connected with the mystery surrounding the number seven. To increase the number of planets under consideration from seven to ten is to lose contact with this deeper wisdom. Under such circumstances it is justifiable to go back to the original system of seven major planetary bodies. These are, after all, the only ones which can be seen with the naked eye.

The seven planets of the ancients, (which incidentally include the Sun and Moon as 'planets') correspond to seven archetypal patterns of possible influence within the human psyche. The descriptions of these are as follows.

1) The Sun.
Light giving, warmth, source of life, transcendent power, daytime, creative force.

2) The Moon.
Bonding, maternal, clasping, sleep bringing, vague,

fluid, sensitive, dark, receptive, cold.

3) Mercury.
Quickness, wit, versatility, details, factual memory, communication skill, shallowness, daftness, flippancy.

4) Venus.
Emotion, love, desire, beauty, refinement, fashion, decoration, artistic sense, the muses, foppishness, sloth, charm, meekness, patience.

5) Mars.
Violent, aggressive, forceful, destructive, pushy, drive, disciplined, valour, zeal, brute strength, anger.

6) Jupiter.
Fullness, success, liberality, the rule of law, acumen, mastership, the long view, conservative, organised, pomposity, gluttony, experience, vulgarity, optimism.

7) Saturn.
Death, inner vision, intelligence, understanding, pre-occupation, restraint, denial, failure, disgrace, dogged-ness, perseverance, melancholy, asceticism, pessimism.

It can be seen from this table that these seven archetypal influences fall into three distinct pairs of opposites with one left over on its own. Viz: Sun and Moon, Venus and Mars, Jupiter and Saturn. The seventh member of the set is Mercury, which corresponds with the colour green, the central colour of the spectrum.

Whilst most people are aware of their own birth-sign, the sign of the zodiac occupied by the Sun on their date of birth, most are ignorant concerning the planetary archetypes. This is strange because in many ways these are much easier to see in terms of everyday life. The archetypes give rise to psychosomatic tendencies to which we are all subject. In each of us there is a blending of the fundamental patterns represented by the archetypes with one or two more predominant and quite recognisable as traits of both looks and personality. We are therefore able to follow tradition and draw up thumbnail sketches of the seven fundamental planetary types and these should be recognisable as factors making up the characters of everyone we know.

The seven types are:

1) The solar type.

These are of medium height, have a darkish complexion, a rather round face and a tendency to grin a lot. These people are usually rather generous with their advice and forthright in expressing an opinion. They radiate a confidence in themselves which others either find attractive or infuriating depending on their own views. Solar people like to be seen, enjoy and audience and treat life like a stage. Emotionally they tend to be rather insecure, usually because they go out of their depths with the wrong people. They are often very poor judges of character and are easily won over by false modesty and flattery.

Ronald Reagan is a typical Solar type.

2) The Lunar type.

The typical lunatic is rather small and has pale skin which is easily burnt by the Sun. They tend to have small, triangular faces, wide eyes and small chins. These people love being unconventional both in attire and in behaviour. They tend not to have fixed opinions about things but adopt whatever ideas come to hand that day. Their main preoccupation is with emotions, relationships and vibes. These are the people who won't let go of bad emotional experiences and bore their friends with interminable analyses as to why some relationship went wrong ten years earlier. Though unconventional, these people usually have good business acumen - largely because they are so sensitive to other peoples radiations. This makes them good judges of character and situations.

Felicity Kendal is a typical Lunar type.

3) The Mercurial type.

These people are usually small and very light boned

with youthful features and tastes even when old. They are extroverts who love gossiping and meeting new people. Others like them for their wit, friendliness and the breath of fresh air that they bring. They often have remarkably good memories for trivial details and odd bits of useless information but this is balanced by the difficulty they have in grasping concepts and the deeper implications of their knowledge. They excel in professions that require constant contact with the public and therefore make good salesmen, interviewers, actors and comedians.

Cliff Richard is a typical mercurial type.

4) The Venusian type.

These people tend to be well proportioned in youth, though with a tendency to run to fat in middle age. They are often strikingly good looking with beautiful faces, skin and allure. Academically, Venusians are usually not all that bright but this is balanced by artistic talent and abilities whether these be expressed as art, music, literature or the stage. These people are fond of luxury and they dote on children and pets. Their chief weakness is laziness and an inability to keep appointments but they usually make up for this by their charm and easy going manner.

Marilyn Monroe was a typical Venusian type.

5) The Martial type.

Though usually less than average in height, these people make up for it by their drive, aggression and purposefulness. They are stocky in build with heavy bones and often rather coarse features. They are quick to get angry and very impatient with the weaknesses of others. Their drive, stamina and determination often leave other types in awe. These people love discipline and are at their best when following routines or working tight schedules. They regard all other types as lazy incompetents but if not carefully controlled themselves, they are liable to do more damage than good. For this reason they make better lieutenants than commanders.

Sean Connery and Margaret Thatcher are both typical Martian types.

6) The Jovial type.

These are of average height but are characterised by their large heads, which in the males are often bald. These people tend towards stoutness even when quite young. By the time they reach middle age they are almost invariably overweight. They make good merchants, bankers, councillors and judges as they combine a keen sense of what is possible coupled with what is both practical and traditional. They are shrewd in business but usually quite liberal towards those working under them. They love to surround themselves with the trappings of success and will often patronise the arts, even when these are meaningless to them personally. They are noted for their good sense of humour and generally jolly disposition.

Chancellor Kohl is a typical Jupiterian type.

7) The Saturnine type.

The typical Saturnian is tall and thin with powerful, deepset eyes and a large jaw. These people are the deep thinkers being drawn to science rather than art, theology rather than rhetoric. Saturnians have penetrating minds and faculties and tend to look for connecting principles rather than to collect factual information. They have a commanding, if sometimes sinister, presence and a strong sense of destiny. These people are prone, particu larly when young, to long bouts of depression. This is especially so if they think they are failing their destiny. This can give rise to a dark sense of humour and a pessimistic outlook on the world. If not actually ascetic, the average Saturnian has little interest in luxuries for their own sake. This when taken to extremes can lead to a miserly disposition.

Norman Tebbit and Clint Eastwood are typical Saturnian types.

Whilst it is true that all of the 'planets' work at different times through everyone, nevertheless there will always be a predominance of one or two in any given individual. It is quite clear that there are Saturnine, Martial, Jovial etc. people, all of which are recognisable as types. The skill in life is to learn to become adaptable and not to be fixed always into the same pattern of behaviour.

By studying the planetary archetypes and making a close study of oneself, it is possible to see how one's own behaviour is conditioned to acting nearly always in one way. It is as though one has a spotlight always shining through the same colour filter, whether this be blue, red, green or yellow. One needs to recognise the planetary archetypes at work inside the psyche and to see how these bring both talents and deficiencies of character. It is then that one can seek to make best use of whatever special aptitudes on has whilst striving to overcome the negative shadow of that same planetary archetype. Thus Solarians must learn humility; lunatics must learn to forgive; Mercurians must learn honesty; Venusians must learn to be industrious; Martians must learn compassion; Jovians must learn austerity; and Saturnians must learn fellowship.

Within any organisation, be it a company or nation, there is always a mixture of different types, which when taken together blend to give a totality. Problems arise when one type gains dominance over all the others and prevents the other types from giving expression to their skills as well as their negative traits. The very Martian Mao Tse Tung virtually destroyed the Jupiterian, merchant class in China - with dire consequences for the material welfare of the country. Equally the saturnine Ayatollah Khomeini, overthrew the 'Sun kingdom' of the Shah, and initiated a regime based on ascetic repression. The entire feminine side of the Iranian nation was repressed into unconscious-ness, with the result that the most barbarous atrocities were able to be committed without any feelings of shame, remorse or pity. This led to a falling back into barbarism worse than the original dictatorship of the Shah.

Fortunately such extreme examples as these are rare. Yet

the principle holds true even within such small units as the family. Personality clashes are nearly always related to differences in predominant planetary archetypes. Recognising the strengths in others and the weaknesses in oneself is the first stage in the development of balance in the psyche. If this seems an unobtainable goal, then so be it. It is at least a worthwhile objective and even small successes will bring large dividends and a more harmonious life.

CHAPTER 3

Medicine and Astrology.

The subject of Astrological pattern and influence has only ever been one aspect, although an important one, of the mystical philosophy concerning the stars. However, Astrological symbolism has been applied in many different areas of study as a means of shorthand and a way of systematising and relating diverse phenomena.

One such area is medicine where it was at one time recognised that disease in the human body is the result of imbalance or distemper - a lack in temperance. The word temperance changed its meaning in the 19th century and became identified with the notion of abstention from intoxicating drink but earlier, during the Middle Ages, it was understood that a temperate man was one who was balanced, who kept his temper. Our English word temper comes from the Latin verb *temperare* meaning to mix. Thus a temper is, properly speaking, a mixture and not a flash of anger. We still use the word in this older way when we talk, for example, of 'tempered steel', which refers to a particular mixture of iron and carbon.

The mediaeval view of medicine was not concerned with microscopic organisms as the source of infections, for they were unknown at that time. Rather the physician would seek to treat the body as a whole and thereby return it from its distempered state to one of correct temperance. The underlying philosophy of medicine at that time was the theory of 'humours'. There were considered to be four humours in the body called respectively black bile, yellow bile, blood and phlegm. These were normally in a state of balance, though with a slight predominance of one or other which gave the individual their characteristic temperament.

Should this delicate balance be disturbed, then the person would be bad-tempered or ill-humoured. The four normal temperaments resulting from the predominance of a specific humour were given the names:

Phlegmatic - predominance of phlegm
Choleric   - predominance of yellow bile.
Sanguine   - predominance of blood
Melancholic - predominance of black bile.

A phlegmatic person is one with an easy, amiable nature but naturally lazy and tending to indolence. They are rather lethargic with a lack of ambition and drive. Physically they have a proneness to chest troubles and frequent colds, catarrh and other lymphatic excesses. However, these people very rarely get angry and are usually sympathetic to the problems of others.

Choleric people are the very opposite of phlegmatics. They are the 'angry young men' of this world. They have drive, ambition and a craving for success come what may. They are quick to get angry and often get into fights. Their typical complaints are liver and stomach disorders, especially painful ulcers. They are also particularly prone to diarrhoeas, fevers and pestilential infections.

The third group, the sanguines, are the typical 'good livers'. They tend to be round. red faced, jolly people. They are the ones who seem to have everything going for them and are great opportunists and judges of people and situations. They are prone to systemic disorders including heart and kidney trouble, strokes and obesity.

The fourth group, the melancholics, are the lean, hungry sceptics. Though tall and thin, they are often surprisingly strong and robust. They are generally serious, deep-thinkers with few real friends and are prone to frequent bouts of depression. Their chief ailments are constipation and related illnesses from retaining too much poison in the blood. These include headaches, joint pains, back pain, arthritis and associated discomforts.

The four humours can be applied to four of the

planetary types, the correspondence being as follows:

Phlegmatic - Venus
Choleric   - Mars
Sanguine   - Jupiter
Melancholic - Saturn

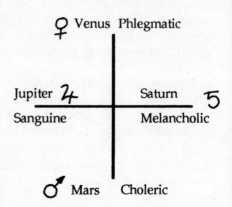

They can also be shown diagrammatically (along with their planets) as two pairs of opposites placed on the four arms of a cross.

The four humours are also related to the four states given the names: cold, dry, wet and warm. All eight can be put together on the following diagram.

This very useful diagram shows the affinities and dissimilarities between the humours in terms of elemental dispositions. For example, both choler and melancholy are 'dry' humours, but one is cold and the other hot. If one were using this system as a means of prescribing suitable treatments for

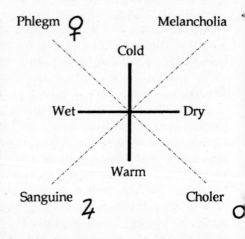

excess of one or another humour, then one might consider a cold bath as suitable for an excess of choler and a hot bath for excessive melancholy.

The diagram of the humours and planets is, however, incomplete. There is firstly the central point of the cross to be considered and then a possible third axis that passes through this centre perpendicularly to the plane of the existing cross. Symbolically, the central point corresponds with the planet Mercury and the new axis links the two qualities of 'Sun' and 'Moon'. We therefore arrive at a diagram like this:

The central point of the diagram represents the quality of temperance, that is exact balance between the four humours on the one hand and a harmonising of the qualities of Sun and Moon on the other. These latter two fac-

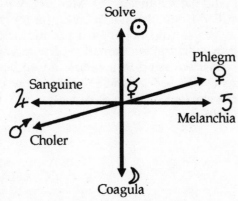

tors are traditionally named as Solve and Coagula or dissolution and coagulation. Just as a humming top can be spun by pushing a plunger up and down, so the tension between solve and coagula can be said to drive the circulation of the four humours.

It was this sort of esoteric reasoning that was the foundation stone of mediaeval ideas of physiology and it was the identification of the planet Mercury with the central point of temperance that led to the adoption of the Caduceus of Mercury as the insignia of medical science. It was always the intention of the physician to restore his patient to a state of temperance, which could be achieved by balancing the two symbolic serpents, the one solve in nature and the other coagula, that were twined around Mercury's caduceus or staff.

If all of this seems fanciful to the modern mind then it should be remembered that in our modern science of medicine it is recognised that the vegetative state of the body is directly determined by the relative balance between the two halves of the Autonomic Nervous System, the one called the Sympathetic the other the Parasympathetic. Stimulation of the Sympathetic corresponds with the process of solve whilst stimulation of the parasympathetic corresponds with coagula. Probably ninety percent of drugs other than antibiotics derive at least some of their effect from stimulating one or other of these systems. So the symbolic Caduceus of Mercury with its twin serpents is still very much alive in 20th century medicine.

We should not regard Chemotherapy as a final solution however, for we cannot really be called genuinely healthy whilst we need to swallow an endless supply of pills. The real aim of medicine should now, as always, be to re-establish natural balance in the body, a true state of temperance.

CHAPTER 4
Alchemy and Self-Transformation.

It is common knowledge that our modern science of Chemistry has its roots in the older 'pseudo' science of Alchemy. The Mediaeval alchemists with their retorts,furnaces and dusty textbooks were only the latest of a long line of serious seekers for the elusive art of transmutation. The work of the metallurgist or smith has always been shrouded in a certain aura of mystery and to become a master gold, silver or even black smith entails a long period of apprenticeship. To extract gold, silver or copper from the dust of the earth and then to turn this into articles of either spiritual or secular usefulness is indeed an art, even though it is one we often take for granted today.

It is not really surprising that many of the techniques of Chemistry should have been kept secret. The knowledge of smelting, tempering and fashioning iron, for example, was the equivalent in the ancient world of nuclear physics in the modern. Those who knew the secrets of metals brought power as well as wealth to their rulers and indeed we classify the history of the ancient world into the periods of the golden age, the bronze age and the iron age.

We think today of Alchemy as a fool's quest to make gold out of lead. Almost certainly this was a later development of the tradition. Alchemists in the earlier days were probably trying to do no more than to extract precious metals from mineral ores. Now there are several points to be considered here, if we are properly to understand the significance of Alchemy and the early alchemists. The first of these is the contrast in status between the smiths of say the Greek period and the modern worker at a blast furnace. Whereas the steel workers of today have a fairly humble status in the community, the smiths of the ancient world were at the very forefront of technology and had considerable influence. It was they who fashioned the bronze and later the iron weapons that gave the edge in battle and therefore ensured the success of their patrons and the security of the states in which they lived.

The extracting of mineral ores and then their re-blending to make specialised alloys has always been an important task within any civilised community and in ancient times was the chief concern of specialised initiates, who were taught the various processes and secrets of the art. The rich and the powerful then, as well as now, wanted more gold than they could either afford or was available in the market place. There are only two ways around this problem, either you have to steel it from someone else or you have to manufacture substitutes from other metals. The simplest way of increasing the amount of 'gold' you possess is to mix it with equal parts of silver to make 'electrum'. This was done frequently in ancient Egypt. An alternative substitute for gold is brass. This has the advantage that the raw materials are relatively cheap but the disadvantage that unlike electrum it tarnishes. In both ancient and mediaeval times the search for a blend of metals that could be transmuted into real gold was certainly a serious pursuit and not considered to be the hopeless task it is today. The tedious work of practical Alchemy was a respectable occupation, for the discovery of a workable formula would bring wealth and fame to both the alchemist and his patrons.

This, however, is not the whole story of Alchemy, for it also developed as a metaphysical system in its own right. This may have been a later development or it may have been a secret part of the art all along, we cannot tell. What is clear is that the stated goal of most alchemists was not the manufacture of synthetic gold but rather what was called the "gold of the philosophers". "The elixir of life" or simply 'the philosophers' stone'. All genuine alchemists are at pains to point out that their work is no ordinary transmutation of the elements but concerns some secret process of a philosophical nature, one which they are not permitted to reveal openly. A full discussion of the symbols, riddles and practical techniques of philosophical alchemy clearly lies outside of the scope of the present volume. We are after all concerned with Astrosophy not Alchemy. However, as certain alchemical ideas have a bearing on what is to follow, a discussion of some of its basic philosophy is clearly worthwhile.

The most famous text dealing with philosophical Alchemy is the *Tabula Smaragdina*, or 'Emerald Table' attributed to Hermes Trismegistus. This was originally written in Greek, though the earliest versions we have are Arabic translations of the original Alexandrine text. This, when retranslated into English is as follows:

'True, without deceit, certain and most true.

What is below is like what is above and what is above is like that which is below, for the performing of the marvels of the one thing.

And as all things were from one thing, by the mediation of one thing: so all things were born of this one thing, by adaptation.

Its father is the Sun, its mother is the Moon; the wind carried it in its belly; its nurse is the Earth.

This is the father of all the perfection of the whole world.

Its power be integral if it be turned into Earth.

You shall separate the earth from the fire, the subtle from the gross, smoothly and with great cleverness.

It ascends from the Earth into the Heaven, and again descends into the Earth and receives the power of the superiors and the inferiors. So thus you will have the glory of the whole world. So shall all obscurity flee from thee.

This is the strong fortitude of all fortitude, because it will overcome every subtle thing and penetrate every solid.

Thus was the Earth created.

Hence will there be marvellous adaptations, of which this is the means.

And so I am called Hermes Trismegistus, having three parts of the philosophy of the whole world.

What I have said concerning the operation of the Sun is finished.

This remarkable work has been the source of speculation and wonder for centuries. The 'one thing' which is mentioned in several places is what was termed in Greek *pneuma* = meaning breath, spirit or ghost. The translation into English is not precise because we really have no equivalent word. What *pneuma* means is a special, fine 'substance' that vivifies or gives life to something. It is a hidden property, yet one which is all important. In Alchemy the *pneuma* was closely identified with what is termed mercury or quicksilver (quick meaning living in old English). The Emerald Table concerns the work, or *opus*, of freeing and binding *mercury* by means of alternating processes of *Solve* and *Coagula* = dissolution and coagulation. Something of the seriousness of this mystery is conveyed when one realises that the Greek words *Pneuma Hagion* are translated into English as 'Holy Ghost', the third person of the Christian Trinity. What the text is saying is that both Heaven and Earth are created by the condensations of *pneuma*, that this universal breath is the elemental substance from which all is created.

This is a difficult concept for modern minds to grasp but if we substitute the word *energy* for *pneuma*, then we come near to understanding what is being spoken of in the Emerald Table. Energy, in its widest sense, is what is called the 'one thing', mercury, quicksilver, Hermes or breath. The importance of this Alchemically is that energy is able to undergo transformations without itself being either created or destroyed. The *Opus* of Alchemy is therefore one of transforming energy. It entails the separation of energy from the gross and the fixing of it into the subtle. Science has long realised that the transformation of energy is the key to understanding how the universe ticks. There is one glaring omission, however, in the way that the science of energy transformation is generally taught in school and university. This is the way that science only treats energies in a quantitative way and fails to recognise qualitative differences. It is assumed that because primordial energy is interconvertible, that all energies are basically the same. It is not generally recognised that there is a scale of energy types and that within this scale there are qualitative differences between energy types. These differences relate to what might be called the degree of order within the energy type or, alternatively, the degree of freedom and 'fineness' of activity associated with the energy in question.

To take but one example, there is a qualitative difference between the energy of heat and the energy of electricity. The latter is a 'higher order' of energy than the former and this is the reason that whilst electrical energy can be converted to heat with near 100% efficiency, the reverse is not true. It is as though in financial terms electrical energy is a hard currency whilst heat is a weak one that nobody really wants.

The process of going from a more disordered, coarser energy state to one that is higher and finer is called an 'evolutionary' transformation. The reverse process of degrading the fine to the coarse is called 'involution'. Alchemy makes use of both processes, but its final goal or purpose is the building of the philosophers' stone, a crystallisation involving energies in a very refined or evolved form.

Before considering the more esoteric applications of this doctrine, we can perhaps digress slightly and discuss some of the energy transformations that happen in an 'apparatus'

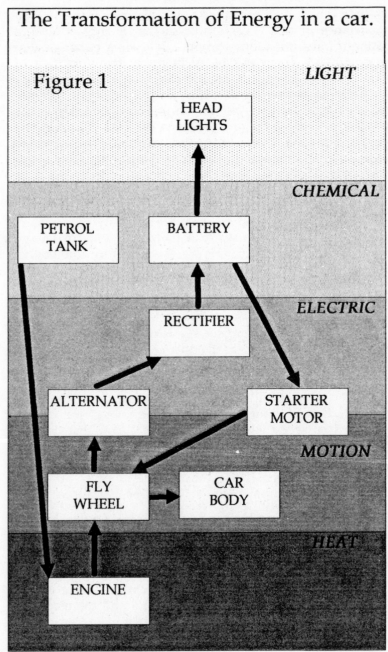

The Transformation of Energy in a car.

Figure 1

LIGHT

HEAD LIGHTS

CHEMICAL

PETROL TANK

BATTERY

ELECTRIC

RECTIFIER

ALTERNATOR

STARTER MOTOR

MOTION

FLY WHEEL

CAR BODY

HEAT

ENGINE

familiar to all of us, the motor car. Here we have a very special mechanism which is designed to transform the chemical energy stored in petrol and air into the energy of motion of a vehicle and its passengers. The processes of energy transformation within the car are typical of those encountered in a range of diverse machines including the human body which, considered from the mechanical point of view, is no more than a vehicle itself. What needs to be understood is that the various energies that are transformed operate on different levels. The car itself is a collection of two kinds of apparatuses:

a) Those which are concerned with energy transformation.

b) Those which are concerned with energy storage.

By taking into account the differences in energies and also considering the mechanisms of transformation and storage by level, we can arrive at a schematic diagram for the workings of a car (Figure 1)

It can clearly be seen that the running of a car depends in the first place on the availability of the correct fuel in the petrol tank. The fuel is then vaporised, mixed with air and burnt in the engine. This process is the first major transformation and it is involutionary in its nature. The petrol-air mixture is degraded to become exhaust gas and heat is liberated. As the gas burns. so it increases in pressure and this pressure change is used to drive the pistons. This is the second major transformation of energy in the car and it is evolutionary, for mechanical energy is 'higher' than the random , molecular movement called heat. It is this double transformation of chemical energy to heat and then heat to movement which is the driving force of the car.

In the case of the old-fashioned steam locomotive, which is an analogous though simpler machine, these are the only two transformations involved. However, the car is more sophisticated and requires electrical energy for the production of sparks, to drive the starter motor and to work the accessories. Therefore, in order to keep running, the car needs to constantly replenish its reserves of electricity. This is accomplished by a third energy transformation, again evolutionary in nature, which takes place in the alternator. Here some of the mechanical energy of rotation is converted to A/C electricity, which is an electrical wave motion. To turn this into D/C requires a fourth transformation and this is carried out in the rectifier.

In order to store electricity a battery is needed. However, what is stored is not electricity itself but rather chemical energy in a form that can be readily converted back to electrical energy when needed. This means that there is a fifth evolutionary step involved in storing electrical energy as chemical potential in the battery. It is interesting to note that the chemical energy stored in the battery is at roughly the same level as the original energy stored as fuel in the in the petrol tank. Yet it takes five steps to go from petrol tank to battery and the efficiency of conversion is very low after so many evolutionary steps in between.

The various accessories of the car which are driven by electricity mainly entail involutionary processes. However, there is one further evolutionary process worth mentioning. This takes place in the various lamps where electrical energy is converted into light. Light is at a higher level than even chemical energy. In fact it is the sunlight that was originally captured by plants which is stored as chemical energy in petrol. The energy that leaves the car as light has therefore gone full circle in a process lasting millions of years.

There are two other processes that need to be considered to make the system complete. The first of these concerns the way that chemical energy in the battery can be turned back into electrical energy and then used to drive the starter motor. This is the reverse process of that which takes palace in the alternator and it involves an involutionary change from chemical energy to the energy of motion. Secondly as anybody who has ever had a flat battery must know, there is also the possibility of starting the car by pushing it. In this case the energy of motion is transferred directly to the car body by the person doing the pushing and this motion can in turn be taken up by the moving parts of the engine to set it going. It should be noted that recharging the battery from the mains is also an outside intervention, though this draws on an external energy source at a higher level than that of muscular effort!

It was pointed out earlier that in some respects our physical bodies are like cars. Of course the human body is vastly more complex than even the most expensive car but it remains true that we depend upon transforming the energy contained in food to carry out the functions of life. This was well known to the Alchemists and they used the symbols of the seven planets to describe and disguise their knowledge of human nutrition. It is the Alchemy of the human body that was of prime interest to them, not the manufacture of metallic gold. The system given here is not complete but it is enough to show what the process of Alchemy was all about.

The seven planets, as used in Alchemy, represent seven densities or materialisations of energy. These were each symbolised by a metal, the seven metals chosen being those most commonly used in the ancient world. The allocation of metals to planets was as follows:

Gold	- The Sun
Silver	- The Moon
Mercury	- Mercury
Copper	- Venus
Iron	- Mars
Tin	- Jupiter
Lead	- Saturn

Just as we were able to follow the various transformations of energy in the car, so also can we follow equivalent transformations taking place in the various machines, accumulators and equipment that make up the totality of the organism we call 'man'. The transformation of energy in man begins with the food we eat. The totality of what passes through our mouths to enter the digestive tract makes up the *prima materia* of alchemical transformation in the body. This is acted upon by the various digestive juices in the first 'furnace' of the stomach. The sediment or slag passes out through the bowels whilst the essential nutritious quality of the food, symbolised by the first alchemical metal lead, passes into the blood stream.

The second transformation takes place in the liver, which operates as a highly sophisticated chemical factory. Blood containing food absorbed from the stomach and gut must first pass through the liver before it can go anywhere else in the body. The function of the liver is both to remove any harmful toxins that may have been ingested and to turn the raw food into a form that can be used by the other organs and cells of the body. This is a process analogous to the manufacture of petrol (gasoline) from oil. Alchemically this process is one of turning lead into tin and it is significant the astrologically the liver is always said to be ruled by the planet Jupiter.

The third process takes place in the lungs and involves both the oxygenation of blood and the transformation of matter into 'life force' or vitality. It is not just a matter of taking in oxygen and eliminating carbon dioxide but rather of building up the magnetic quality of the blood. Breath and life are closely interrelated and breathing involves the uptake of many subtle emanations and vibrations in addition to the physical process of filling the lungs with fresh air. The quality of the atmosphere we breath is very important to our well being and has a deep affect upon the psyche. There are places upon the Earth where the atmosphere is rich in 'psychic nutrients' and where we can't help but feel better and conversely there are other places where it is so depleted and poisoned that it causes severe depression and all manner of psychic as well as physical ills. The life force that animates our blood is symbolised in alchemy by the metal iron, the one which gives blood its red colour. Too little iron and we feel sleepy, lethargic and lacking in vitality too much and we are restless, aggressive and overly 'martial'.

The fourth transformation is that which turns the vital energy of the blood into *eros* or libido. It is wrong to say that this transformation takes place in the genitals. They use rather than generate this energy, for it has application throughout the entire body and is absolutely necessary for effecting healing in the case of injury and for regulating the processes of the body. It is intimately bound up with the autonomic nervous system and seems to be manufactured throughout the body in all of its cells, though it is concentrated in the nerves. This energy is symbolised in alchemy by the metal copper and the planet Venus, named after the goddess of sexual regeneration. It is, of course, closely related to emotional moods, feelings of desire and the sexual urge.

The fifth transformation concerns the transformation of *eros* into nervous energy, that which allows us both to sense and to be sensitive to our environment. This energy is largely made at night and finds its place of manufacture in the cerebellum at the back of the head. Such faculties as sight, taste, hearing and touch depend upon the correct manufacture and use of this energy. It is also the chief energy required by our brains to carry on the tasks of computing, memorising and reasoning. This energy corresponds in alchemy with the metal quicksilver or mercury. It is the energy that gives quickness of mind, wit, flexibility and ordinary intelligence.

The sixth metal is silver and this corresponds with the energy of imagination, the ability to make mental pictures or 'thought forms'. There are very few people today who are able to make much use of this energy and what little we have at our disposal is usually wasted in day-dreaming. The increased manufacture and control of this energy was one of the main preoccupations of the ancient alchemists and would have enabled them to perform many so called miracles.

The seventh metal is gold, the metal of the Sun and this energy is responsible for the power of self-consciousness, sense of individuality and above all the faculty of 'will'. Metallic gold does not tarnish in the atmosphere of planet

Earth, so it has always symbolised the incorruptible, that which is timeless and therefore able to bring about a sense of being outside of time. We could compare this energy with the light generated by the headlights of a car. Just as it is possible for a car to run without ever using its own lights, so also it is possible for a person to live their life without eve really experiencing the energy of 'gold'.

The seven energies, as represented by the seven planets or metals are at work in us all of the time, though for the majority of people these processes are not under their own control. Any silver or gold that may be manufactured accidentally is usually consumed as fast as it is made. The work or *Opus* is to speed up the production of higher energies, a process known as sublimation. To do this requires knowledge, discipline and sacrifice as well as help from others who have trod the way before.

To conclude our brief survey into the mysterious world of bodily alchemy, we can look at one last diagram. This relates the planets and their metals with the signs of the zodiac that they rule. It symbolises the way that the year is a cyclical process of evolution followed by involution. There is a steady process of evolution from the dark, leaden winter to the time of summer when the fruits of silver and gold may be picked. After the time of Leo, there is a process of involution throughout late summer and autumn as energies invert back towards Saturn - lead. This diagram, though very simple has profound meaning and warrants careful study. It may even go some way towards explaining the strange illustrations, often found in alchemical texts, of the trees that bear the fruits of Sun and Moon.

The Cycle of the Metals

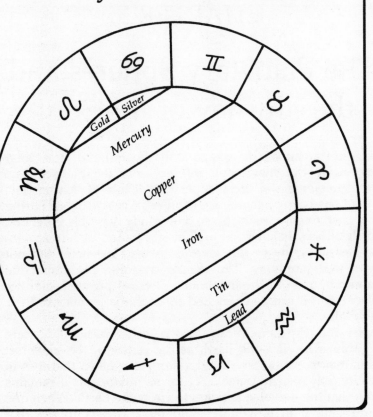

CHAPTER 5

The Planetary Spheres and the Journey of the Soul.

To discuss either the shape and dynamics of the Solar System or the angles and influences of the planets is to touch on only the most superficial levels of Astrosophy. There has been a resurgence of interest in Astrology during the past twenty years or so but rarely has this extended further than the charting and interpretation of horoscopes. To restrict study to this level is to read the notes but not hear the symphony. The deeper meaning of human life cannot be read in the inanimate, physical processing of the planets yet it can be expressed through the potency of their symbols.

In the Pre-Copernican Era it was considered quite legitimate to view the Earth as the centre of the universe. This may seem rather a bold assumption given that it is in reality only a small planet. Yet for its inhabitants it remains true that the universe appears to circle the Earth. When one thinks about it, it would be no more correct to say that either the Sun or the core of the Milky Way is the centre. In terms of objective, measurable physics, we have no real conception of where the centre of the universe may be, or even if it has one. Why not, then, let the Earth symbolise the centre. That at least corresponds with the human viewpoint!

Using an Earth centred model, we can devise a system of orbits for the planets as they circle it. If we call the Sun and Moon 'planets' (for the benefit of what follows), then we can organise the Solar System according to distance of orbit or the planets from the Earth. Going from nearest to farthest we have a system as roughly as follows: Moon, Mercury, Venus, Sun, Mars, Jupiter, Saturn. This was the classical system of ordering of the planets and for this reason does not include the orbits of Uranus, Neptune and Pluto which were not discovered until relatively recently.

Seen from the Earth, the planets appear to wander north and south of the Ecliptic. In fact their progress often seems quite erratic, like insects walking on a spherical glass window. In classical times each planet was associated with its 'sphere', a sort of invisible glass bubble on the surface of which the planet travelled. The entire conception of the universe was not just of planets orbiting the Sun but rather of a Solar System consisting of shells within shells, like Russian dolls, one within another. Beyond the sphere of Saturn was the sphere of the fixed stars, what we would now call the Celestial Sphere and that marked as it were the very boundaries of existence.

The more hidden teachings concern the planetary spheres than the planets themselves. Just as the modern Celestial Sphere is conceived of as rotating about the extended axis of the Earth, so also the individual planetary spheres rotate about this same axis. In fact the north-south axis that stretches from the pole star, through the physical Earth and down to the south celestial pole is conceptually the axis of the universe itself. This doctrine of the universal axis is the meaning behind many religious mythological symbols. It has been described obliquely as the axis of the spinning top of heaven, the vortex of the great maelstrom, the central pivot of the world 'mill' and (most commonly), as the trunk of the universal tree.

In the Scandinavian sagas this tree is called Yggdrasil, the holy ash. It unites the three worlds of Heaven, Middle-Earth and Hell. Within the Judaeo-Christian tradition it is the 'Tree of life' that dwells in the midst of the Garden of Eden (Gen. 2:9) which is later, at the very end of the bible, to be placed in the midst of the New Jerusalem (Rev. 22:2). It is noteworthy that in revelations the tree is described as having twelve kinds of fruit, one for each month. This again brings us back to the zodiac and the way that the twelve signs rotate about the world axis. The traditional symbols of the Christmas tree, maypole and the fairy-tale beanstalk are all allusions to the world tree, the axis of the spheres. The story of Jack and the beanstalk concerns the second property of this tree, that it can be climbed. This teaching is seen most clearly in the mystical Jewish Kabbalah. In Kabbalism the diagram referred to as the tree of life unites several different esoteric teachings into one shorthand format.

Kabbalah is a complex doctrine, most of which was transmitted orally from master to pupil and not written down until about the fourteenth century. The most important part of this teaching centres around a diagram representing the tree of the universe that stands between two pillars, identified with the twin pillars of Solomon's temple (1Kings 7:22). Placed on the diagram are the ten sephirot or lights that are said to be the prime creation. The sephirot can be considered Astrosophically to relate to the nine spheres (from Earth to zodiac) plus one more that represents the primum mobile or first movement.

The creation of man is said to come about by a process of descent along a zig-zag path through the sephirot. This is in a sense a descent through the spheres from the absolute, through the zodiac and planetary spheres, to incarnation on Earth. A full discussion concerning the kabbalah is obviously well beyond the scope of the present work. What is important is the light it throws on astrosophical thought as preserved in the Hebrew tradition. The descent of the soul through the planetary spheres is a doctrine held by many different schools and religions. The process of incarnation is considered, from the spiritual standpoint, to be a steady and progressive falling into matter. The soul first enters the zodiac and then passes through the decreasing astral spheres, to be finally born as a helpless baby. Having been born, the soul must then go back by a reverse process of life to the point where it can step back into the void and pass out of the astral spheres.

Certain understandings of this doctrine have passed

The Planetary Spheres and the Kabbalistic Tree of Life

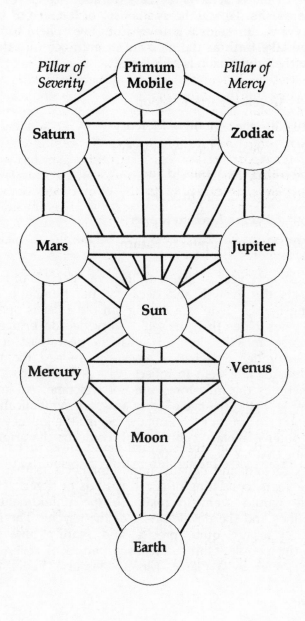

down to us in what might be called colloquial wisdom, though the origins of this wisdom have been largely forgotten. One such is the understanding that the greater cycle of life is of seventy years duration, i.e. seven periods of ten years. To use the symbolism of the tree of life, each ten years represents a journey from one sphere to the next. If we take birth as the moment of entrance into the Earth, then the progression is as follows:

0 - 10 years, Earth to Moon

10 - 20 years, Moon to Mercury

20 - 30 years, Mercury to Venus

30 - 40 years, Venus to Sun

40 - 50 years, Sun to Mars

50 - 60 years, Mars to Jupiter

60 - 70 years, Jupiter to Saturn.

The seventy year of life, with its seven periods of ten years, reflects the growth and decay of the human body as a living being. There is a saying 'an old man is one who is ten years older than oneself'. Every decade brings with it remorse for the loss of what is now past and new opportunities in what is emergent. Indeed the ten year periods of life seem to reflect very definite stages, though sometimes the milestones are not welcome. An additional point is that at the age of forty a person symbolically passes beyond the orbit of the Sun and begins the journey through the outer planetary spheres. This could be the origin of the saying that life begins at forty.

A second and equally important cycle is that of forty nine years, consisting of seven periods of seven years. This cycle would seem to relate to the unfoldment of the faculties and the development of the psyche. The stages in this cycle are quite precise and readily observable in healthy people. Once more each period of seven years is ruled over by a planet: Moon, Mercury, Venus etc. The development of the cycle is related very much to the way that the 'psychic force' is directed, what C. G. Jung calls 'libido' (in the broadest sense of the word). During the period from birth to the age of seven the child forms a conscious mind. In the earliest years the barrier between reality and fantasy is thin, which is why this is the age of fairy-tales, witches, Santa Claus and all the magic of the nursery. For very young children the difference between what is physically real and what is imagined is hard to distinguish. This is because they are still half in the dream world, the world symbolised by the sphere of the Moon.

At age seven we say that the child has reached the 'Age of Reason'. School work (which was play) now becomes much more serious. There are important skills to be learnt, knowledge to be absorbed, rules to be obeyed. Children of this age become fascinated by dinosaurs, museums and the natural world. A more recent discovery has been the way many children of this age group have a natural facility when it comes to handling computers. Their ability to grasp the basics of computer programming often leaves their parents bemused. Children of this age group also tend to take up hobbies such as collecting train numbers, stamps, coins or anything else that can be catalogued, checked, evaluated and numbered. All of these are functions that relate to the sphere of Mercury, the second in the series of seven.

Come fourteen and there is another big psychic change that must be gone through. The interest in trains, stamps and games is suddenly overwhelmed by a new interest, sex. Puberty is one of the periods of greatest stress in a person's life, for the sexuality of youth is immediate, constant, usually unsatisfied and very demanding. It is not just the embarrassment of seeking a first kiss or caress that must be overcome but rather there is the crying need of the personality to find acceptance in the eyes of its own peer group. Not only must the boy or girl strive to be attractive to the opposite sex (a single pimple can be extremely upsetting) but they must also conform to the fashion of their peers. Usually this takes the form of rebellion against the older generation of their parents and this gives rise to the weird hairdos, aggressive posturing, outrageous closthes and the idolisation of pop-stars who embody the fashionable image. All of this behaviour comes under the sphere of Venus, the classical goddess of sex and love.

At twenty one there comes the symbolic key to the door. At last one is able to come and go as one pleases without the necessity of parental permission. The dominant phase now, however, is under the rulership of the Sun and this brings fresh problems to the fore. The first of these is the question of "who am I and how can I find myself?".It is no longer enough to be part of a peer group and even sex cannot satisfy this new thirst for identity. What is calling out is the voice of the ego, personified by the young and handsome Sun god Apollo. The seven years from 21 to 28 are sometimes called 'provisional adulthood' and can witness the most selfish behaviour. It is the time of the ego and the crisis of identity, often accompanied by many changes of home, job and lifestyle. It is usually during this period that person seeks for the help of a guru or teacher, a wiseman who's council can be trusted by the emerging ego. Similarly this is the time when political, religious and philosophical questions seem of the greatest importance and when opinions are formed on all of these matters.

The change at twenty eight is not as well documented as those earlier. The dominant sphere is now Mars and this injects a new energy and purpose into life. The psychic life moves on from its preoccupation with 'being', with the identity (and vanity) of the ego. There comes a reassessment and a realisation of how much time is slipping by. The imperative now is to go and 'do' things. It is a time for will and discipline, a time for bold changes and new responsibilities and these in turn often involve considerable self-sacrifice. It is not enough anymore just to be, the individual now has an overwhelming urge to make a mark, whatever the personal cost. It is under this influence that early marriages often break up, for Mars is intolerant of fools and quite ruthless in clearing up the mistakes of the past.

In contrast, the period from thirty five to forty two is usually considered the most rewarding in life. This is the time when the psyche opens to the sphere of Jupiter, often called the 'Greater Benefic' in Astrology. Jupiter is the planet of destiny and authority, symbolically he is the father of the gods. During this middle period of life there comes the flowering of the seeds sown in youth. The psychological outlook is one of benevolence compared with the irascibility of the martial years and there is a sense of authority, expansiveness and optimism. This is the time when ambition can at last be realised and a professional peak attained.

The final period of this forty nine year cycle relates to the flowering of Saturn and is possibly the most mysterious of all. Symbolically Saturn is identified with the Greek god Chronos, the god of time. If Jupiter has brought success and authority then this is challenged by Saturn. The psychic outlook under Saturn looks beyond the present to the future. What is of concern now is how to turn the success of the present into a lasting legacy. The desire now is to create a dynasty or enduring legend of oneself. the urge being to outstrip time before death claims all. To do this entails a certain sacrifice of the present in order to make way for the future. Typically, at this time a man might turn his private business into a public company. (though still carrying his name) so that others will run it after he dies. Alternatively he may take his own son onto the board and hand over much of the executive function to him, again preparing for the future.

It is difficult to say whether we are justified in continuing this cycle further. Perhaps there are more spheres that should be considered that would relate to the more recently discovered planets of Uranus, Neptune and Pluto. If so then this would be a new departure. Classically the planetary spheres ended with Saturn and after this lay the sphere of the zodiac and the fixed stars. Another way of looking at the whole cycle is to say that each sphere is like a bell. It rings loudest during those periods of life that correspond with its own sphere, yet it keeps echoing that sound for the rest of life. Sexuality, for example, does not end at the age of twenty one and neither does the desire for knowledge at fourteen! It would seem that the psychic faculties are opened one after the other, at seven year intervals, and thereafter remain open till near the end of life. Looked at in this way one can truly say that the peak of life is at fifty, the age at which all of the psychic faculties are fully open and receptive.

Before ending this chapter, there is one other point worth considering. This is the question of whether or not the opening of the psychic faculties is automatic in all people. It is very clear that brain damaged children are usually incapable of making much progress in the development of many of the mental faculties, i.e. those relating to the sphere of Mercury. Equally many others never develop the sexual awareness of Venus or the sense of ego of the Sun. We may surmise then that the opening of the psychic faculties at seven year intervals is the ideal and not necessarily the reality. It is not a guaranteed process and in fact seems to get harder the further you progress up the scale. Many remain dominated for all of their lives by the faculties represented by the inner spheres of Mercury, Venus and the Moon and this could be the reason why the transitions at twenty eight and later are less well recognised than those marked by the age of reason, puberty and majority.

IV

Religion and Astrology

CHAPTER 1

Ritual as a Cosmic Drama.

In an earlier chapter, attention was drawn to the importance and relevance of church orientation and the canonical ordering of both the ecclesiastical calendar and the times of daily prayers in accordance with natural astronomical time-cycles. However, the involvement of religion with Astrosophy goes much deeper than this. In fact all major religions have always been closely associated with starlore, whether this has been a straight forward matter of belief in Astrology or a deeper, more esoteric application of cosmic symbolism. This is scarcely surprising as the main function of religion is to provide man with a channel to the Godhead, the Being(s) we consider not only responsible for our own existence but also that of the universe in which we live. The great vault of the heavens, whose cyclic rotation measures out the steady rhythm of time, is ever the prime mystery of creation. In whatever way we speculate and try to explain away its majesty, we can never really escape its challenge to our own inflated self-importance. Perhaps the greater heathens are not the atheists, who though dismissing God as unknowable yet still seek to understand the laws of the universe, but rather the many modern evangelicals who are happy to dismiss the cosmos as of no account.

The Christian religion, more than most, is infused with astrosophical insights and this right from its inception. After all, was not Jesus' birth signified by the star of Bethlehem? Was he not visited even in his cradle by the wise men of the East, the star-gazers of Persia? This event alone should make any Christian pause to think, for if stellar portents were considered important enough to be written down as confirmatory signs of his royal birth, then surely anyone wanting to be called a Christian had better not turn a blind eye towards the stars.

Much ancient star-wisdom has been either completely lost or has taken forms which are now so far removed from their point of origin as to be unrecognisable. The early church did not take root, as it were, in virgin soil. It became established in lands with long and deep traditions of their own, some of whose cultural insights we are only now beginning to appreciate. It is therefore not so surprising that many ancient cosmic ideas were adopted and adapted by the early Christian fathers to give substance and authority to what, at that time, was a small, heretic cult. We must not forget, however, that there were many fresh concepts born of the Christian age itself and that these have taken root in the symbols, ceremonies and rituals of the church. Most of these, such as the Mass and 'Way of the Cross' have a cosmic significance of their own. If they had not then they would not have lasted for nearly two thousand years.

All genuine, religious formulations contain inner truths and understandings which are not immediately apparent to the uninitiated. The great art of symbolic expression is not that the symbols themselves have to be more complex in order to express deeper wisdom. Rather the power of symbols lies in the way that they can cause connections to be made in the inner, subconscious mind. The degree to which this can happen depends upon the breadth of education and the degree of inner development of an individual, for if the mind itself is empty of suitable contents, then connections cannot be made.

An example of this sort of communion is poetry. If one does not speak or understand the language in which a poem is written, then all that can be appreciated is its rhythm, tonality and possibly mood. Where the words are familiar to the listener, then a communication of ideas can take place as well. Yet not all in hearing the same words will truly understand the poem, for so much depends upon previous experience, semantics, knowledge of poetic formulae and precedents. Just as poetry has depths of meaning, so also do religious formulations, sacred architecture, prayers and rituals. To be effective and meaningful these have to conform to the laws of nature and supernature. The practice of religious ritual is itself an act of high drama, for the priests, acolytes. choir and congregation are united in the performance of a mystery play. The purpose of such plays is to bridge the worlds, to enable the soul to receive nourishment not given to it by the world of everyday life. Indeed the Latin word for pope is pontifex, or bridge-maker and this is a clear description of just what his function is supposed to be.

Within the Catholic Church the central ritual is the celebration of the Mass or communion feast. The most sacred moment of the Mass is when the priest utters the words "This is my body", the words first uttered by Jesus at the last supper. When these words are repeated by the priest, the bread is said to have been transubstantiated into the body and blood of Christ Himself. The priest then solemnly raises the host above his head to show it to the gathered congregation. This act, an important part of the ritual of the Mass can be seen to equate the rising host with the rising Sun. The body of Christ is believed by Christians to be the source of light, power and life in the spiritual world in just the same way that the Sun is in the physical. The equation of host and Sun goes even deeper than this relationship between parallel worlds, for bread is not only a symbol of life but actually IS the staff of life. Bread is the produce of the Earth, the vessel of the living light sent by the Sun. Without bread we would die. In the communion host we see united the symbols of the rising Sun and the harvest of the Earth as man's nourishment. Until very recently it was the practice that the priest should actually face East during the Mass with his back to the congregation. Thus when he raised the host above his head, there would have been morning sunlight streaming in through the east window to illuminate his act. The whole drama would then have had an added dimension of realism, the Host as the Son of Light on Earth illumined by the power of the heavenly light of the Sun.

After the priest has raised the host he consecrate the wine also and then raises the chalice. Just as the host parallells the rising of the Sun, so the chalice can be seen to correspond with the rising Moon, the heavenly body which influences the tides of sea and ocean. The sea is water, the second principle, without which there would be no life. Through the processes of life water can become grape juice and this in turn can be fermented to make wine. Wine symbolises the blood, the inner river of the body and the carrier of the life force. Thus we see that the two symbols of bread and wine are charged with cosmic meaning for those with the eyes to see. Yet even this is not the full meaning, for there is also within the Mass an act of faith. The bread is no longer bread, it is the body of Christ. The wine is no longer wine, it is the blood of Christ. To the ordinary mind such words have no meaning, for clearly there is no perceptible change in chemical composition of either the bread or the wine. We need to remember that this is an act of high drama and the bread and wine are principle actors.

The success of a dramatic performance depends upon suspension of disbelief, for the actors and actresses must no longer be thought of in terms of the personae of their everyday lives but must take on the roles that they are playing. In a good production of Hamlet, for example, we lose sight of the actors as themselves and commune with them as the characters they play. They are no longer Lawrence Olivier or Audrey Hepburn but perhaps Hamlet and Ophelia. Through the skill of the actor the past and even the future can be brought to life in the present and the audience is given the opportunity to experience events that take place outside of their own time and by this means gain insight, knowledge and emotional sustenance. It is this added dimension of drama that brings to religion its supernatural quality. Without this it becomes a matter of cold buildings, stale bread and stuffy atmospheres, a mere "conjuring of bones" to quote the bishop of York. The Mass is only one example of such drama but even private prayer and meditation can be greatly reinforced if supported by ritual.

In the last section of this book we shall look deeply into the religious, astrosophical symbolism. It may then be possible to speculate further on the esoteric meaning of various teachings and practises in ways that bring a breath of fresh air into what is often a dull, boring subject. It is likely that some of the ideas written here may seem highly unorthodox or even heretical. However, we have a duty to look deeper than ever before into these mysteries because unless new and more powerful formulations of the truth can be found, western civilisation will degenerate totally into a state of ignorant barbarism. Man cannot live by bread alone, he needs contact with spiritual truth. For such contact to be made requires that first a chasm be spanned. Cosmic symbols form a suitable ladder or bridge between the worlds of heaven and Earth.

CHAPTER 2

Worlds of Revelation.

It was pointed out in an earlier chapter that the cruciform structure of churches derives not just from a pious remembrance of the crucifixion of Jesus but from a certain awareness of the importance of time. By orientating the church upon the rising Sun, so also the other three quarters of the day are marked by the nave and transcepts.

This idea of quartering finds other expressions within the church that have direct astrosophical associations. At Wells cathedral for example, the famous twenty four hour clock not only has hands on it showing the positions of the Sun and Moon at any given time but also has painted into the four corners of the clock face the symbols of the four evangelists. There are many illuminations in the British Museum and other libraries of the world similarly showing the four evangelists engraved in the four quarters of a page around the central figure of Christ upon his throne. The symbols used for the four gospel writers come from the Book of Revelations, the last book in the bible.

The astrosophical symbolism is clear as the four beasts depicted are the zodiacal signs marking the fixed corners of the ecliptic and therefore by inference the four seasons, the four quarters of the day and the four phases of the Moon. The following table shows the relationships between evangelists, beasts, seasons and zodiacal signs:

Season	Fixed Sign	Evangelist	Beast
Spring	Taurus	Luke	Bull
Summer	Leo	Mark	Lion
Autumn	Scorpio	John	Eagle
Winter	Aquarius	Matthew	Man

It can be seen that the only major discrepancy is autumn (fall), which is normally symbolised by the scorpion. The time of Scorpio is, however, linked with not only death but self-sacrifice. In this context it can be likened to the phoenix that martyrs itself to attain transcendency. The great mystery of religious practice is the transformation of the base, lower nature to something higher. The desire filled lower nature is often symbolised by a serpent that slithers on its belly and stings like a scorpion. Conversely the higher nature is symbolised by the eagle, the king of birds that can fly higher than any other. The eagle is the symbol of transcendency over the serpent and is related to the deepest and most secret side of religion and initiates the world over understand the symbolism of the eagle clutching the serpent in its talons as it flies back to its eyrie in the distant heavens. St John's gospel is the most esoteric of the four and he is symbolised by the eagle with its clear and penetrating vision rather than the lower scorpion which as a symbol represents only the lower manifestation of Scorpio, the dark before the light.

In the Book of Revelations it is said that the four beasts that sit around the throne each have six wings and are full of eyes all around and within. Day and night they never cease to sing Holy, Holy, Holy is the Lord God Almighty. Here again the visionary writer of Revelations is using astrosophical symbolism and an understanding of this symbolism raises this image from one of pious reverence to a meaningful description of the eternal creation. If we consider that each beast represents one quarter of the zodiac, then each wing corresponds to one twenty-fourth of the cycle, the amount turned in one hour of the day. The eyes that fill the beasts within and without are clearly the stars, those within being the stars of the zodiac and those without being the rest of the stars that make up the heavenly sphere. The great hymn that is sung day and night is a recognition of the power emanating from the throne of God around which the entire heavens are seen to revolve. The implication of this verse is that the turning of the spheres is something sacred, the obedience of the angels to the Will of God, and expresses the Glory and thanks of the creation towards the source from which it springs.

The four corners of the celestial sphere are marked by the fixed signs of the zodiac and there are similarly four fundamental directions as marked by the four chief points of the compass. There is a correspondence of phase between the fixed seasons of the year and the four, basic compass points. In the northern hemisphere winter corresponds with north, summer with south, spring with east and autumn with west. This is interesting because the Christian symbols for the four evangelist have a clear earlier precedent in ancient Egypt. There it was customary, when burying a mummy, to first remove the viscera and put them separately into four special jars, which were then packed into a chest and put close by the coffin. The stoppers of these four jars were depicted as the heads of the four sons of Horus (the Egyptian sky God). These sons of Horus were the genii, or lesser divinities, related to the four points of the compass = north, south, east and west. Egyptian religion was permeated through and through with animal symbolism, which in its later and more degenerated forms became superstitious animal worship and magic. However, the four sons of Horus closely parallel the later, Christian symbols for the evangelists. The Egyptian gods were: Duamutef, the jackal headed guardian of the stomach; Qebhsenuef, the falcon headed guardian of the intestines; Hapy, the ape headed guardian of the lungs; and Imsety, the human headed guardian of the liver.

Not only were the organs of the deceased Egyptian to be guarded over by these four protective deities but the four jars were themselves identified with the four goddesses Neith, Selkis, Nephthys and Isis (who represent midnight, midday, dusk and dawn respectively). It is probable that the Egyptian practice of placing the viscera into four separate jars and then bringing the jars together into one box was symbolic of calling back his lost vital force from the four corners of the universe so his powers of digestion and breathing would not be lost to him in the next world. It may also have been symbolic of uniting the four cardinal directions and the four times of day and thus in a sense of transcending space and time, a prerequisite for entering the realm of eternity. The aim of immortality is to go beyond time and matter and this can be symbolised by including all of time and every direction. In a sense this is analogous to the eternal song of the cherubim that carries on day and night Holy, Holy, Holy is the Lord God Almighty .

Revelations itself is a difficult book to understand. It brings together a number of threads and weaves them into a tapestry of great complexity. The language used is a combination of cryptic coding and dreamlike symbolism. These combine together to give an awe inspiring vision of what is happening in the unseen world of the spirit. Many of the symbols used are drawn from the earlier books of the Old Testament, in particular from Daniel and Ezechiel. In this sense Revelations can be seen as supplying a further chapter too the prophetic story already presented in these earlier texts.

The interpretation of prophecy, particularly of the sort of apocalyptic visions given in Revelations, is never an easy matter. Those who are interested must be prepared to make a detailed study of not only the Old and New Testaments but also of Middle Eastern history. They must also study symbolism and in particular the way that certain symbols are elaborated and developed in the course of the biblical narrative. This, as it were, throws light from different directions onto the same subject matter. For the benefit of the present work, it is sufficient to look at Revelations from the perspective of astrosophy.

Revelations Chapter IV. which introduces the four beasts, also describes the throne of God in a Mandalic image. The implication is that just as the Earth is considered to be at the centre of the physical universe, so in the unseen world of the spirit there is a central throne of God. Thus just as the visible Earth is often surrounded by a rainbow, so this throne is also circled by one, though of emerald. Similarly, just as the dry Earth borders the sea, so this throne has before it a sea of glass, the invisible ocean of space. As for the seven torches of fire (called also the seven spirits of God) these can be compared with the seven planets that travel through the zodiac. The whole image that is developed in this chapter is one based upon the theory of correspondence between Heaven and Earth, 'As above, so below'. The image of heaven loses much of its force when taken out of context and separated from the doctrine of correspondences.

Cosmic symbolism is continued further on in chapter XII. Here a portent is described of a woman, clothed with the Sun, the Moon under her feet and on her head a crown of twelve stars. She is described as about to give birth to a male child who will rule over the Earth with a rod of iron. Not unreasonably this passage has always been interpreted as portraying the Virgin Mary, both as the prospective mother of the infant Jesus as the Queen of Heaven. However, the symbolism speaks for itself, for she is described in cosmic terms which are only applicable to the Earth herself. It is the Earth that is 'clothed in the Sun', (for the light and warmth of the Sun fills the whole atmosphere) and the Moon does symbolically lie at her feet. The twelve stars of her crown symbolise the twelve signs of the zodiac. Thus the image implies that this woman is the incarnation of the Great Earth Mother herself, that she is the Queen of Heaven made flesh. This mystery is alluded to in the central prayer of veneration for the Virgin Mary, the 'Hail Mary'. In Latin the first two words of this prayer are 'Ave Maria', which has a secret meaning. First of all Ave is the name of the ancient Celtic goddess of the Earth (she gives her name to such places as Avebury and to the many rivers Avon to be found in Britain). There is also a pun intended for A-V-E spelt backwards gives E-V-A, the Latin name for Eve, the first woman and the 'mother of all things'.

It is very interesting to compare the symbolism of Revelations XII with the story of Isis, the great goddess of the Egyptian pantheon. She also is depicted as Queen of Heaven and just as the incarnated woman of chapter XII is later pursued by a terrible dragon bent on destroying her and the child she is to bear, so also was Isis (as the mythological queen of Egypt) pursued by Set, the principle of evil and the murderer of her husband Osiris. The parallel goes further for Isis was to give birth to Horus, the child of Osiris who was to avenge the death of his father and reestablish the rule of law upon the Earth. We can therefore see that the prophecy contained within Revelations XII harks back to a much older archetype, the myth of the Queen of Heaven (Isis) made flesh, whose son would one day rule the world and reestablish the reign of his heavenly father on Earth. This suggests that John of Patmos, who wrote the Revelations was inspired by a perennial, archetypal vision.

In Chapter XXI there is the description of the New Jerusalem, the heavenly city of the new age which is to come. This again is a cosmic symbol, an archetypal pattern which exists in the unseen rather than the description of any physical city. It is described as having a high perimeter wall with twelve gates. At each gate there is an angel and over each is inscribed the name of one of the twelve tribes of Israel. The pattern of the wall is taken from the zodiac, the twelve signs corresponding to the twelve gates and the twelve tribes. In verse twenty one the gates are compared with pearls, each gate corresponding with a single pearl. Oysters and the pearls they contain are traditionally symbolic of the Moon, so it can be seen that this is an allusion to the lunar cycle, there being twelve lunations to the lunar year. The vision of the holy city is completed with a description of the Tree of Life with its twelve fruits, one for each month of the year. This is, of course, the archetype of the universal axis of the physical universe, known to the Scandinavians as Yggdrasil, the sacred Ash Tree.

To explain Revelations in astrosophical terms one must see that the hidden world of the spirit has more than one level. In fact in the visions of St. John four distinct 'worlds' are described. The first of these is what might be called the Palace of God. This is the Mandala image of Chapter IV, the place of endless praise where God has his throne. The second is Heaven, what we would perhaps call the Astral

World, the place where the souls of the dead take up their abode. Most of the drama in Revelations takes place at this level in symbolic form and is depicted as a contest between Good and Evil. The eventual goal of Revelations as described in Chapters XXI and XXII is the setting up in heaven of the New Jerusalem, the spiritual abode of the saints.

The third world is that of the Earth, that is to say the world of flesh and blood, the material universe in which we live. Finally the fourth world is the Abyss or underworld which we would call Hell. This is described as a prison and it is here that Satan is to be held bound for 1000 years.

The descriptions of all of these worlds are taken from the archetypal image of the Cosmos, the hidden worlds being described in terms analogous to the visible. Even the symbol of the dragon as the embodiment of evil has an astrological connection, for the constellation of Draco, the dragon, is circumpolar and dominates the night sky. Thus the dragon is connected with the image of darkness, the power of the night. The binding of the dark dragon is symbolic of establishing the rule of law. It is the suppression of the dark and primitive urges that would otherwise topple the empire of light.

Such ideas as these are deep and profound and are perhaps best left in the language of Revelations itself, for the mystery of dualism and the war between Light and Dark can only be resolved through deep contemplation. It would clearly be wrong to trivialise such matters. What is clear is that it is time that this book was opened and read, for it seems to have buried within it an important message for our times. For are we not the generation born under the shadow of the bomb?

CHAPTER 3

Some Fishy Parables.

To anyone not acquainted with the subject, it may, at first sight, seem strange to suggest that there are references concerning the study of Astrology to be found in the New Testament. We are used to hearing Astrology lumped together with witchcraft, divination, magic, spiritualism and all the other damnable devices which are roundly condemned from the pulpit. Yet a closer study of the Bible shows that Astrology has always played an important part in religion. What is damnable is the corrupted form that it took in the later Babylonian and Egyptian empires, a form which was based upon superstition and the abuse of esoteric knowledge as a means of obtaining personal power and manipulating situations to the wrong ends. An analogy would be the abuse of a doctor's clinical records. These, when used by the doctor as a reference in the diagnosis and treatment of his patients, are a valuable and important part of his overall system of healthcare. However, should these documents fall into the wrong hands, then they could be used negatively, e.g. for purposes of blackmail. For the confidential record's of a person's illnesses are also records of their weaknesses, be it high blood pressure or mental illness.

Astrology was considered to be the highest of the sciences in the ancient world. It was not much concerned with the casting of horoscopes or the sort of ridiculous predictions made in todays newspapers. Rather it was more like a system of 'weather forecasting' of what might be termed the psychological climate. It was understood that the relationship of Sun, Moon and planets at any given time has a direct effect upon the atmosphere and causes such feelings as elation, depression, jingoism, stagnation or apathy. At any given time there is an 'atmosphere' which affects what today we might call the collective unconscious. It was the job of the astrologers of old to identify the prevailing influences and to advise both the ruler and the people how best they should react in the given circumstances.

Within any real religion there is always an exoteric or outer teaching concerning what is considered sufficient to give guidance for the living of ordinary life, and an esoteric or inner teaching for those with the ability and determination to look deeper. The artistry of the parable was, and is, its ability to convey different levels of meaning at one and the same time. The New Testament is full of Parables and it is recorded that Jesus often only explained the full meaning of these to his immediate disciples. The parables are not the only New Testament examples of exoteric teaching overlaying the esoteric. It must be remembered that at the time the Gospels were being written, there were no printing presses and all books, parchments or scrolls had to be copied by hand. Economy of style was called for and what was written in the Gospels was not a simple biography of Jesus and his teachings. Rather they were intended as working documents, based loosely about the major events of his life and written in such a way that each story would have multiple levels of meaning.

To make a full study of these writings could take a lifetime and even then the esoteric meaning of any particular episode can easily be missed simply because to see it requires education in a subject as seemingly unrelated as mathematics. Yet very clear evidence of esoteric teaching can be seen, particularly in the stories of the miracles. One may or may not believe that miracles actually took place, what is clear though is that the way they were written up was intended to convey other levels of meaning than the simple story itself. One such miracle that clearly has an esoteric, mathematical interpretation is the miraculous draft of fish. This is discussed is some detail by John Michell in his excellent book *CITY OF REVELATION*. His interpretations of this miracle are based on gematria, the study of the correspondence of words and numbers. This was a favourite method of coding used by both Hebrew and Greek scribes. Although this system need not concern us here, it is clearly an important detail in the story that the number of fish caught is given as exactly 153.

This number seems meaningless and rather absurd until it is realised that 153 is both the product of 9 and 17 and also the sum of all the numbers from 1 to 17. It seems unlikely that the choice of the number 153 was chance, what seems more likely is that there is some hidden meaning being expressed here. One way of interpreting this is to imagine that there are 153 snooker balls. These can be arranged to form a triangle in the same way that the ten red balls are set up in their frame at the start of a game of snooker. Where there are only ten balls, these are arranged in four rows of 1,2,3 and 4 balls respectively. We can therefore say the 10 is the 'triangle' of four. This way of arranging 10 is known as the tetractys and was very important both as mathematics and as an esoteric theorem in the philosophy of Pythagoras. We can therefore see that the 153 fish caught in the net could well be a reference to the tetractys of 17. By joining up diagonal dots, a net is produced and this, with the associated mathematical and geometrical symbolism implicit in this shape may well have been used as an esoteric teaching aid in the earliest Christian study groups of the Apostles.

Another miracle, or perhaps it should be said pair of miracles, that clearly have an esoteric meaning is the story of the feeding of the five thousand. This miracle is described in more or less the same words in all four gospels. In each case the setting is the same. Jesus has been preaching to the people in the midst of a desert. He realises that they are hungry but the only food that is available is five loaves of bread and two fishes. Accordingly he orders the people to sit down on the ground and then breaks the bread and fish and gives it to his disciples to distribute. After the meal they are ordered to pick up the fragments left over and these fill twelve baskets. In all five thousand men have been fed excluding women and children.

This version of the miracle is more or less the same in all four gospels. In addition there is a second, similar miracle described in two of the gospels, Matthew and Mark. This time there are only four thousand men, there are seven loaves plus a few fishes and only seven baskets of fragments are left over. To emphasise the importance of an inner meaning to these miracles, in Matthew:16 Jesus calls attention to the numbers involved. He contrasts the feeding of five thousand with five loaves and the feeding of four thousand with seven loaves. He also makes clear a further level of interpretation when he states that bread is not to be taken as meaning food but as doctrine, that is to say religious teaching.

If we look more closely at the wording of the miracle of the feeding of the five thousand as given in Matthew:14, this will become clearer. There are certain contradictions in a literal interpretation. First of all it is said that he led the multitude into the desert but then in verse 19 it is said he commanded them to sit on the grass. The same thing is said in Mark:6 when they are commanded to sit on the 'green' grass. The disciples also suggest first of all that maybe they should go into the surrounding villages to buy bread, until they realise that they couldn't possibly afford to buy enough to feed such a multitude. Since grass doesn't grow in a desert and it would also seem unlikely that there would be permanent villages in such a place, it is evident that we are to understand the term 'desert' in a symbolic way. It is a place that is without sustenance for the spirit not for the body.

The bread and fishes are also to be understood as symbolic of his teaching and wisdom. In general terms we can say that he is able to 'feed' the people through his disciples. He breaks bread and gives it to his disciples to disseminate to the multitude. This we can take as meaning that he instructs a small group himself and they are then able to go and teach the many. In this way the bread is increased a thousand fold. The story also has a twist at the end of it which is characteristic of esoteric teaching, for it is said that the disciples are sent to pick up the scraps left over and these fill twelve baskets. Since there are twelve apostles. it is evident that the twelve baskets represent them. We can interpret this as meaning that in the process of instructing the people, the apostles take his words and are enabled to reach new understandings and wisdom themselves beyond what they are actually teaching exoterically. This higher level of teaching the multitude are not able to assimilate and it becomes a gift for the apostles themselves. Anyone who has ever done any lecturing themselves will know what is meant here. Often the teacher learns more than the student.

If this were all that we could grasp from this miracle, then it would already be a great deal, however, we must also take into account the symbolism involved in the numbers of people, loaves and fish. Although the two different miracles differ in detail, there are certain similarities that we can take note of. In the first version there are five loaves and two fishes. In the second there are seven loaves and no fish. In both cases the number seven is either implied or stated. The same is true of the numbers of people. Version one gives the number at five thousand and number two at four thousand. On both occasions we are given the numbers in terms of thousands.

Numbers are often used symbolically in the scriptures and it is therefore worth examining them in some detail. The number 1000 can also be seen as equalling 10 cubed.

Thus the number 1000 contains the idea, whether intentional or not, of three dimensions. We can visualise 1000 as a cube of side 10. If we do then 5000 would relate to five such cubes. The most obvious way to organise five cubes is in the form of a cross. Four such cubes can be arranged in a square. Although such numerological interpretations are speculative they are not beyond reason.

Esoterically there is a relationship that can be drawn between the loaves and fishes and astronomy. In one version of the miracle there are seven loaves and in the other five loaves and two fishes. The loaves would have been circular in shape whilst the fish would correspond to the shape known as the Vesica Piscis. In the version of the miracle where Jesus feeds (teaches) the people with seven loaves alone, he is instructing them at one level. Where he feeds with loaves and fishes, he can be said to be teaching on tow different levels, the fish representing the more esoteric.

It is well known that the number seven is frequently observed in natural phenomena. In general it can be said that seven of something makes up a group class of manifestation. There are for example seven periods of elements in the periodic table, seven crystal classes in the mineral world and the seven colours of the rainbow. When white light is passed through a prism it splits into the seven colours which make up the essence classes of light that make up the group system we know as colour. White light is a blending of all the colours together. Because of this they cancel out one another and the colour of white light is neutral. For the colours to be seen they must first be

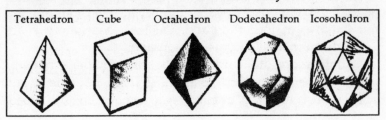

Tetrahedron   Cube   Octahedron   Dodecahedron   Icosohedron

differentiated, which is the function of the prism.

It is the same with other groups of essence classes, for example minerals. In order for a rock to crystallise, it must take on the geometry of one or another of the seven crystal systems. It cannot be all of them at once and it has to be one of them or it cannot crystallise at all. The division of groups of similar things into seven essence classes is one of the central teachings of most esoteric systems both old and modern. As we have seen, this understanding is particularly evident in the Book of Revelations. The text is written in the form of an encoded letter to the seven churches in Asia of Ephesus, Smyrna, Pergamos, Thyatira, Sardis, Philadelphia and Laodicea. These churches form seven essence classes that taken together symbolise the group of the whole church, just as the seven colours make up the rainbow.

Other essence classes described are the seven golden candlesticks, the seven stars in the hand of the Son of Man, the seven lamps of fire before the Lord, which are the seven spirits of God, the seven seals on the Book of Life, the seven horns and the seven eyes of the lamb that was slain, the seven angels that stand before God, the seven heads of the dragon Satan Etc..Later it is pointed out that the seven candlesticks are the seven churches themselves and the seven stars are the seven spirits ruling over these churches. This gives us a direct indication that Astrology is considered to be important. The seven stars from the very earliest times have been understood as the same ones after which we have named the days of the week, namely the Sun, Moon, Mars, Mercury, Jupiter, Venus and Saturn. These seven form an essence class with a direct influence on human affairs.

There is here another peculiarity, which represents a deeper understanding of the way that nature works. This is that any essence group of seven can be divided into a group of five which can be called mundane and two which are in some way higher or more special. Sometimes it can happen that the two special cases are unknown and not even considered at all. In these cases it may appear that the group is complete at five. One such example is the group of Platonic solids. These are the group of five regular figures that can be inscribed inside a sphere so that all faces are equal to all other faces, all edges are equal to all other edges and the points of contact with the sphere are equidistant one from another. The series is composed of:

1) Tetrahedron

2) Cube

3) Octahedron

4) Dodecahedron

5) Icosohedron

Plato was greatly interested in these solids and thought of them as representing five different elements, fire, air, water, earth and ether. Later Johannes Kepler (1571-1630), who drew up the laws of planetary motion, worked hard to find a correspondence between the observed orbits of the planets and the series of platonic solids. Few people have questioned whether or not the series is complete, yet it is evident that as an essence class there should be two more members to make up the whole group of seven. These we would expect to be of a different order to the other five. In fact there are two other regular straight sided figures that can be visualised in the abstract. The first is the sphere itself and the second is the point. The sphere can be thought of as a regular solid with an infinite number of points joined by an infinite number of sides of zero length and therefore with an infinite number of plane faces with zero area. The point is a regular solid with only one point which is joined to itself by zero number of sides with a zero number of faces.

Of course it can be argued that these two do not belong to the series of Platonic solids such as the cube, yet it can also be seen that even though we cannot in practice measure an infinite number of sides of zero length or properly imagine what a solid with zero sides might be like, they do have a mathematical basis for existence. We can see that these two 'lost' solids represent the extremes of the series. The single point is the first member, whilst the sphere is the last. Conceptually we use these figures all the time in thinking about space even though we cannot accurately draw or model them.

Getting back to the essence group of stars thought to have a direct influence on human life, it is clear that these also fall into two distinct groups, one of five and the other of two. The five make up the five planets - Mercury, Venus, Mars, Jupiter and Saturn. The two are the luminaries the Sun and Moon. We can now draw from this an Astrological interpretation of the feeding of the five thousand, which implies that Jesus fed (instructed) the crowd with seven influences, the five loaves representing the five planets and the two fishes the Sun and Moon. The implication is that his teaching has a completeness to it since it incorporated the entire set of psychological types of influence as represented by the seven stars of the ancients.

The teaching given to the five thousand is of a higher nature than that given to the four thousand. In the first case twelve baskets of scraps are filled, whilst in the second only seven. The twelve baskets can be seen as representing the twelve apostles as human astrological types. The twelve signs of the zodiac relate to the Sun/Earth relationship and have a direct reference astrologically to the essential nature of the experience to be undergone by the soul as it comes into incarnation. The seven baskets refer to the planetary set and this astrologically relates to the karma or fate of the individual as opposed to their destiny. It has to be understood here that fate and destiny are not the same

CHAPTER 4

The Mystery Schools and the Way of the Cross.

The connections between modern day Christianity and earlier mystery religions are very often glossed over and certainly never get a mention from the pulpit. This is a pity because far from detracting from the impact of the Christian message, knowledge of its remote ancestors can give added depth to faith.

Long before the time of Jesus, special schools, that promised enlightenment through initiation, were established in Egypt, Greece, Sicily and other places. Many of the early Greek Philosophers, including Hippocrates, Socrates and Plato claimed to be initiates themselves. Such places as Eleusis in Greece and Thebes in Egypt were well known cult centres, though the exact forms of their inner teachings are not known as they were kept as a closely guarded secret. What is known is that the public festivals held at these centres always involved chthonic deities, the gods and goddesses of the underworld.

Each year a dramatic play was acted out at Eleusis on the theme of Demeter's search for her daughter Kore, who was abducted to the underworld by Hades. In the parallel mysteries of the Orphics, the drama was centred around the story of Orpheus, who again searched for his dead wife Euridice, in the underworld of Hades. Similarly, the Egyptian mysteries concerned the murder of Osiris by Set, the magical birth of Horus to Isis the grieving widow and the son's eventual victory over the tyrant usurper.

All of these mystery plays have the same fundamental

pattern, a journey into the underworld leading to confrontation with chthonic deities, judgment and return to the land of the living. It is not hard to see that the plays themselves were only preparatory lessons for the deeper and more secret revelations of initiation. These dramatic stories were acted out to give the candidate extra courage before he too should follow in the footsteps of Orpheus and make his own journey to the underworld.

Initiation itself most certainly involved the candidate going into some form of deep trance state, when his 'soul' would leave the physical body for a time and wander freely in the underworld of spirits before returning back to the body. The trance may have been induced in a number of different ways: by the administration of powerful psychotic drugs, by hypnosis, by yogic practices or through magical invocations.

The principle purpose of initiation was to reveal the world of the dead to those still alive, to prove conclusively that there is life after death. It also offered an opportunity to visit the 'Hall of Judgement' whilst still in possession of a body and therefore able to repent of past sins.

By the time of Jesus, most of the European mystery schools had either died out or become decadent. One notable exception was of course the Druidical schools of Britain, which as they were still outside of the Roman sphere of influence, were still flourishing in the early years of the first century A.D.. Given the secularisation of life in the twilight years of the Roman Republic and at the start of Imperial Rome, it is little wonder that the Gentiles proved to be fertile ground for the new mystery religion of Christianity. However, Christianity could not conquer Rome until it had first defeated its principle rival, Mithraism.

The parallells between Mithraism and Christianity are quite astonishing given that they were rival religions. Whilst, as everyone knows, Christianity was born of the older religion of the Jews, Mithraism was an heretical offshoot of Zoroastrianism, the state religion of Persia before the coming of Islam. Like Jesus, the semi-divine hero

Mithras was said to have been born in a cave and to have received gifts from shepherds. Both religions celebrated 25th December as the birthdate of their teacher, both sanctified Sunday instead of Saturday as their holy day, both used incense, Holy Water, bells and communion bread, and both taught of the struggle between good and evil, the immortality of the soul, judgement day, the resurrection of the body and the fiery destruction of the world at the end of time.

However, whereas Christianity became a state religion and therefore tended to lose touch with its more mystical origins, Mithraism dies out while it was still a small select cult. It only exists now as a fossil record of how it was practised in the early centuries A.D., before its suppression by Constantine. In some ways, therefore, study of its teaching can throw fresh light on what were probably similar practices and rites within the Christian church of the time.

Of particular interest in the present context is the system of Astrological initiations the make up the Mithraic mystery path. Before entering on this path, the candidate had to undergo a period of probation, when he became what was the equivalent of a catacumen in the Christian Church. It is important to note that in the early church, catacumens were not allowed to witness the full ceremony of the Mass and other sacraments. They were taught at the back of the church and had to depart before the Communion service.

For anyone entering the Mithraic path, there were seven degrees through which the candidate could pass. These were identified with the seven planetary spheres and were:

1) Corax   - The Raven, the sphere of theMoon.
2) Cryphias   - The Hidden Master, the sphere of Mercury.
3) Miles   - The soldier, the sphere of Venus.
4) Leo   - The Lion, the sphere of the Sun.
5) Perses   - The Persian, the sphere of Mars.
6) Heliodromus - The Courier of the Sun, the sphere of Jupiter.
7) Pater   - The Father, the sphere of Saturn.

Each initiation represented, as it were, the attainment of a stage, the temptations of that sphere having been conquered. The first stage was symbolic of death to the ordinary world and commitment to the path, the raven signifying death. The second stage was one of intellectual knowledge of the hidden teaching. The third was a struggle with desire and emotional attachments. The fourth was the overcoming of personal pride. The fifth was the development of courage and daring. The sixth was service to the higher principle symbolised by the Sun. Finally the seventh was responsibility for custodianship of the tradition.

Mithraism was certainly intended to be an highly ethical religion, though whether theory and practice always corresponded is debatable. What is interesting is the light that the teaching throws upon the Christian sacraments, which are of course the equivalent Christian steps of initiation. If we identify the seven sacraments of the church with the seven astral spheres, just as in Mithraism, this gives the following correspondences.

1) Moon   - Baptism, the putting behind of Original
                   Sin.

2) Mercury - Penance, Private instruction,
                   confession and paying off karma.

3) Venus   - Marriage, the promise of sexual
                   fidelity.

4) Sun   - Communion, the ritual eating of the
                   spirit of life.

5) Mars   - Confirmation, becoming a daring
                   soldier of Christ.

6) Jupiter   - Holy Orders, ordination of the
                   priesthood as executives of the church.

7) Saturn   - Extreme Unction, the last rites for
                   those passing into the next world.

The connection between the sacraments and the seven astral spheres of the ancients has been lost in the modern church. Confirmation in particular now seems redundant, whilst strenuous efforts are being made to rid Extreme Unction of its death connotations (it is now referred to as the sacrament of the sick). It would be wrong to suggest that the Christian sacraments are borrowings from earlier mystery religions and they are certainly very different from the initiations of Mithraism. Whereas the Mithraic steps were regarded as the rewards of attained status, the Christian sacraments are special blessings for those still on the path. The emphasis is therefore quite different.

The cult of Mithras was one with great appeal to the Romans of the second and third centuries A.D. chiefly because of its emphasis on the need for discipline, standards of good conduct, honesty and the fight against barbarism. It was a religion of the right and therefore favoured by all those who were appalled at the decadence and decline of morals in the empire. In form it bears much resemblance to modern freemasonry and, like the latter, women were excluded from taking part.

The typical mithraic chapel was an underground grotto, reminiscent of the cave into which the god Mithras was said to have been born. Round the walls of the grotto were placed various symbolic sculptures and among these were a set of Bas Reliefs depicting the life of Mithra. Without doubt these would have been important teaching aids for instructing novices in the cult, for most of them would have been illiterate. As everyone knows, a picture is worth a thousand words.

The use of sculpture to describe the central mysteries of religion was common practice throughout the ancient world, with one notable exception, Judaism. The Ten Commandments expressly forbid the worshipping of graven images, and this meant that to place sculptures in Jewish Temple was considered an abomination. This fact alone makes it clear that the use of representational art in Christianity is not derived from Judaism but was adopted from other traditions where this was common practice.

Whilst it is clear that the old craft of sculpting statues in the round found new subject matter in the form of saints and angels, the art of the Bas Relief was not lost either. The early Christians took over this art form but used it in a totally different way from their rivals the Mithraists. Thus rather than imitating the Mithraism and surrounding the church with reliefs on the subject of the life of Christ, these Bas Reliefs concern his death. These are what are known as the stations of the cross and they are to be found in most catholic churches even today. They are fourteen in number and occur in the following order.

1) Jesus is condemned to death.
2) Jesus receives the cross.
3) Jesus falls the first time under the weight of the cross.
4) Jesus is met by his mother.
5) The cross is laid upon a stranger, Simon of Cyrene.
6) The face of Jesus is wiped by Veronica and his image is left on her cloth.
7) Jesus falls a second time.
8) The women of Jerusalem mourn for Jesus.
9) Jesus falls a third time under the cross.
10) Jesus is stripped of his garments.
11) Jesus is nailed to the cross.
12) Jesus dies on the cross.
13) The body of Jesus is laid in the arms of his mother.
14) The body of Jesus is buried in a sepulchre.

The stations of the cross form a system of teaching that is both emotionally powerful and extremely esoteric. Taken superficially the stations are designed to arouse a feeling of remorse and shame for the way that Jesus suffered and died at the hands of cruel men. The stations are both a reminder of his terrible sufferings and of the barbarism of which men are capable. The emotions aroused by meditation on the stations can be enough to bring on feelings of conscience and out of this a new sense of purpose in our own religious endeavours.

However, there are other interpretations of a more esoteric character that can be read into the stations. It is noteworthy that they end in burial in the grave and don't extend to the Resurrection, Ascension and the Last Judgement, as one might have expected. The story of the cross is confined to the tragedy of his suffering and death, the very antithesis of the conquering saviour. This implies that Jesus is here to be seen in his human and not godly aspect, it is the story of a man.

This throws a very different light on the stations themselves and upon their hidden meaning, for it becomes clear that the figure of Jesus is meant to exemplify the fate of all men, for each person that lives must make their own way to Calvary, to their own eventual death. There are 14 stations in all, beginning with the sentence of death and ending with the burial of the dead body. The number 14 was clearly no accident and this suggests that the stations represent a period of fourteen days, which is two weeks or half a Lunar cycle. There is a twofold symbolism implied, firstly the entire period from the condemnation to the burial is symbolised by the decline of the Moon's disc from full Moon to its disappearance or entombment. Secondly it suggests that the journey itself is directly linked to the Moon's influence. Thus the cross born by Jesus could also be symbolic of the cross born by life, the Moon.

Within the narrative, Jesus meets with certain personages and all of these meetings are themselves symbolic. Firstly he meets his mother who symbolises Mother Earth. In the Christian tradition the Virgin Mary is always shown robed in blue, the colour of the Sea and her name Maria is derived from the Hebrew name Mara meaning bitter, the same root as the Latin word Mare meaning the bitter sea. Mother Earth must indeed stand by and watch all her children walk the road of life to their graves.

The second meeting is with Simon of Cyrene, a stranger who is pulled from the crowd and forced to give a hand in carrying the cross. He can be seen to represent the way that other people can give aid in life though even this changes nothing, death is still the eventual destination of all living beings. Without Simon's help, Jesus would never have arrived at the end of the journey but would probably have died in the street. In fact he falls three times on route, which symbolises the close scrapes with death that all people have even before they die. These may be accidents, illnesses from which they recover of other times when the burdens of life just seem too much. Simon therefore represents the friends or even acquaintances who can come into a person's life and help them with their burdens, even though they cannot prevent their inevitable death.

The third person he meets on the way is Veronica, who wipes his face with a cloth. Miraculously his image is left imprinted on it. She represents a loved one, perhaps a wife or girlfriend, whose love is able to sooth, if only a fraction the pain of the journey. Again, mortal love cannot prevent death but it can make life more bearable and those who love us and live on after retain the image of the departed in their memory.

His meeting with the wailing women of Jerusalem is again a reminder that he is not alone in following the road to death, for he tells them to cry rather for themselves and their children who must also in due course die. There is then the nailing to the cross, which can be interpreted symbolically as representing the final agony of a terminal illness. The symbol of the Calvary cross is the very antithesis of the tree of life, for it is the gibbet of death against which all that is mortal must be pinned. The placing of his body in his mother's arms represents the return of mortal remains to the Earth that bore them. The sepulchre in the last station represents the womb of life and death, the secret cave or grotto to which he has now returned in preparation for life after death.

The stations of the cross are, of course, closely associated with Easter and this would explain the oblique reference to the waning Moon as this is the most important Lunar festival of the year. The whole emphasis of the Christian message is one of redemption through the acceptance of suffering as a necessary ingredient of life. By the humiliation of the cross, the Christian is brought to a state where he is able to receive divine grace.

It was the strength of this message and its close

correspondence with the 'spirit of the times' the 'zeitgeist' of the Piscean Age, that ensured the victory of Christianity over Mithraism. Yet by one of those twists of fate and history, even this symbol of suffering and humiliation, the cross, has been used as a banner of war. When one contemplates the obscenities of the inquisition, the crusades and the witch hunting of heretics, one questions whether we have the right to use the word Christian at all. Perhaps a return to cosmic values and a recognition of the Earth's place in the Universe would help redress the balance.

Conclusion

Towards a New Gnosis of the Stars

Throughout the history of man up until modern times, there has been a consensus that both man and universe come ultimately from the same parentage, the Mind of God acting upon the deep void of space. This doctrine is expressed with the utmost eloquence at the start of the Gospel of St. John, the most mystical of the four Gospels. The first act of God is to utter the Logos the'Word', that is to issue a command, to pass a Law, to reach a decision. From this decision, taken in the Deep Mind of God, arises all of creation beginning with the first Light. It is like a stone being thrown in a still pool and causing ripples to go out from the centre. Indeed the Greek word '*arche*', which we translate as 'beginning', really means 'origin' and has more the sense of the centre of a circle, the origin of an arc, than the beginning of the line of time as the English would suggest.

Thus we read:

"In the beginning was the Word, and the Word was with God, and God was the Word. This one was in the beginning with God. All things through Him became and without Him became not one thing which has become. In Him life was and the life was the light of men and the light in the darkness shines and the darkness it not overtook."

These cryptic verses which start the last Gospel are read out at the end of every Mass. They stand apart from all of the rest of the New Testament, like Stonehenge standing in a field of corn. We can see that they allude to some very important concepts, a deep philosophy of creation, yet they seem not to belong to the rest of the New Testament but rather to some older tradition more akin to the first Book of Genesis. It becomes clearer upon further examination that we are dealing with a fragment of a lost mystical teaching.

This teaching in its fullest expression lay beyond what the council of Nicaea sitting in 325 A.D. wished to see taught from the pulpit, yet it couldn't be entirely ignored because as we see here St. John himself had given it his seal of approval by alluding to it at the start of his Gospel. This lost teaching, clearly well known to John and maybe others of the first disciples, was part of tradition generally known as Gnosticism and it has a long history.

Gnosticism was a branch of Christianity most closely associated with Egypt in the 1st and 2nd centuries A.D.. Though later declared heretical in the church councils, it was in fact one of the earliest and most significant movements in Christianity. The Dead Sea scrolls, which were only rediscovered in the late nineteen forties, have shown us that the mysterious Essenes, the Jewish sect most closely associated with both Jesus and his cousin John the Baptist, and from whom many of the earliest followers and disciples came, held many teachings in common with the Gnostics. The Essene brotherhood taught that salvation was to be obtained through personal effort, study and what in the Hindu tradition would be called yoga, rather than the mediation of a priesthood carrying out animal sacrifices in the Temple. For this reason they were at odds with both the Pharisees and the Sadducees who made a rich living out of the Temple.

There were Essene communities in Egypt as well as on Mount Carmel, the site of the former school of Old Testament prophets, and at Qumran on the Dead Sea. It is believed by many that both Jesus and John the Baptist were educated by the Essenes whilst boys and that at least some of the lost years of Jesus' life (between the ages of twelve and thirty) were spent in Egypt studying with the Essenes.

The Gnostic tradition, of which the Essenes represent

one manifestation, go back further than Christianity to the mysterious teacher known variously as Thoth, Hermes and Enoch. He was credited with designing and building the Great Pyramid of Egypt as well as instructing the Ancient Egyptians in matters scientific and mystical. A brief study of the geometry, orientation and fabric of the Great Pyramid indicates that its original purpose was something more than a fancy tomb for a dead pharaoh. The pharaohs were, as a rule buried in the valley of the kings in tombs richly adorned with scenes taken from the Egyptian book of the Dead. There are no murals in the Great Pyramid, no images of the after-life, no remnants of funerary furniture, no Canopic jars, none of the detritus you might expect to find in an Egyptian tomb even after it has been robbed. In fact the only thing ever found in it was a solitary stone coffer. This could equally have contained a hoard of gold coins as the body of a dead king and one might as easily say that the Great Pyramid was a bank as a mausoleum.

If the Great Pyramid was not a tomb, then what was it? Many have speculated on this question but the most common explanation is that it was a temple of initiation. For reasons which we don't understand, it was necessary that it be this shape and size for the work that they were doing. Like all machines, not having seen it in operation it is difficult to guess just what it was used for. There is the common belief though, particularly among modern day writers, that candidates for initiation were taken inside and put into a deep coma so that they could have an out of the body experience and appreciate their own immortal self. Presumably the pyramid shape and the absolute quiet and darkness inside made this easier.

This emphasis on the need for personal experience rather than simply believing a teaching as an act of faith is characteristic of later Gnostic writings and the most important part of this was initiation. It seems that the collection of Gnostic writings that make up what is now known as the Corpus Hermeticum, are in fact records of personal initiations. Thus we read at the beginning of The Poimandres (Libellus I):

"Once upon a time, when I had begun to think about the things that are, and my thoughts had soared high aloft, while my bodily senses had been put under restraint by sleep,- yet not such a sleep as that of men weighed down by food or bodily weariness,- methought there came to me a Being of vast and boundless magnitude, who called me by my name, and said to me, 'What do you wish to hear and see and come to know by thought?' 'Who are you?' I said. 'I', said he 'am Poimandres, the True Mind'."

We have then a sort of Platonic dialogue between the man in a reverie and the 'True Mind', which presents itself to him in the form of an entity called Poimandres. Already one can see the parallells with the experiences of many of the Old Testament Prophets who received many of their prophecies whilst in a state of reverie from similar angelic beings. There is also the similarity with the start of the Book of Revelations, where St. John is similarly thrown into a swoon whilst he is instructed.

The revelation of Poimandres is on a cosmic scale and explains in a most poetic way the dilemma of man, the creature of flesh and blood living on and inhabiting the Earth. We are told that man originated in the realms beyond the stars but that in seeing the beauty of nature, he fell in love with her and she with him. In coming to Earth he took into himself something of the essence of the each of the seven 'governors' or planetary spheres and on incarnating he lost consciousness of his true origins. Unfortunately, though he still had the power of creative action as his birthright, the planetary natures he picked up on his way 'down' through the spheres, tend to act in negative ways. Man himself now has to overcome the temptations of his desirous 'astral' nature and learn to use these planetary influences positively if he is ever to regain his freedom as a spiritual entity.

We see in this story a deep understanding of the opening chapters of Genesis and perhaps something of its original inner meaning. The name Eve, as used in Genesis, means 'mother of all things' and not just the ancestral mother of the human race. We should properly understand her as being Mother Nature. The tree standing in the Garden of the Lord is the familiar 'world tree', the axis of the Universe that we find celebrated in all of the worlds great mythologies and which is the origin of our Christmas trees and Maypoles. It carries on it the many 'fruits' of the stars and planets. The star we put on the top of our Christmas tree is not only the star of Bethlehem but also symbolises the North star to which the axis of the tree points. The coloured baubles represent the different planets of the solar system and one of these is the apple which was offered to Adam by Mother Nature, at the instigation of the cosmic serpent, with such baleful consequences. The apple which carries within itself the hidden pentagram (if you cut an apple horizontally in half the core is in the shape of a pentagram) symbolises the planet Earth. By eating the apple Adam, the cosmic man, took to himself the nature of an animal. He became a cosmic spirit living in the body of a primate. Out of his love affair with nature were born all humans, male and female, who are themselves spirits trapped in the web of life and death and banished from the realm of timelessness, the garden where time does not exist.

For the gnostic, then as now, the way is clear. He must wake up to his true nature and, whilst still alive in his animal skins, discern in himself the planetary 'astral' influences that make up his desire body and learn to control them. We each of us carry within us a seven headed dragon and the names on its heads are avarice, lust, pride, deceit, anger, sloth and covertousness. These are the negative influences of the seven planets Jupiter, Venus, Sun, Mercury, Mars, Moon and Saturn respectively. The Christian yoga is to transform these influences by the alchemy of right living so that they become true to the higher as opposed to the lower expressions of the seven planets, and become the seven gifts of the Holy Spirit.

The gnosis of the stars is that man must learn to distinguish between what we label as 'human nature', that is his planetary and astral being, and his spiritual nature which is his own true being. It is hard to do and our journey is long but ultimately we have no choice but to go beyond this limiting world of nature with its two faces of life and death. It is better to begin the work now than to wait for a trumpet call beyond the grave, for the fulcrum of life is ever the present moment and our 'Now' is the most precious gift we have in this world.

Bibliography

SECTION 1

Positional Astronomy and Astro-Navigation by H.R.Mills.
Stanley Thornes(Publishers) Ltd. 1978
Useful work on measuring star angles and the use of simple astronomical instruments for finding positions of planets etc..

Concise Atlas of the Universe by Patrick Moore.
Mitchell Beazley.
Basic Astronomy and star atlas with many pictures and an outline history of Astronomy.

A to Z Horoscope Maker and Delineator by LLewellyn George.
Llewellyn Publications 1972.
A classic textbook of Astrology covering virtually every aspect of the subject.

Ptolemy Tetrabiblios translated by F.E. Robbins.
Loeb Classical Library, William Heinemann Ltd. 1971.
This is the fundamental classic of pre-Copernican Astrology.

SECTION2.

The Greatness that was Babylon by H.W.F. Saggs.
Sidgwick & Jackson 1962.
A useful account of all the material relating to Mesopotamian cultures.

The Archetypes and the Collective Unconscious by C.G.Jung.
Bollingen Series/Princeton University 1980.
One of Jung's best books with much information on his ideas of the psyche, symbolism, the Mandala and Alchemy.

The Mummy by E.A.Wallis Budge.
Collier Macmillan (London) 1972.
A simple introduction to Egyptology by one of its greatest scholars.

Myth and Symbol in Ancient Egypt by R.T.Rundle Clark.
  Thames and Hudson 1978.
  An intriguing insight into the way symbolism was used in
  Ancient Egypt.

The Timaeus by Plato.
  Penguin classics 1965.
  This is the Platonic dialogue concerning Atlantis and the lost
  arts of measure.

Architecture, Mysticism and Myth by William Lethaby.
  The Architectural Press London 1974.
  One of the most influential books on theoretical architecture
  and its links with Astronomy.

The Canon by William Sterling.
  Research into Lost Knowledge Organisation and Garnstone
  Press 1974.
  A remarkable though difficult book concerning the lost Canon
  of Astronomical Measures and their use in Ecclesiastical
  building.

The Mysteries of Chartres Cathedral by Louis Charpentier.
  Research into Lost Knowledge Organisation and Thorsons
  1972.
  Insights into the hidden canon used in the design of Gothic
  cathedrals, particularly Chartres.

A New Model of the Universe by P.D.Ouspensky.
  Routledge and Kegan Paul 1931.
  A remarkable book in many ways but the chapter on the tarot
  is of particular interest here.

SECTION 3

Deeper Man by J.G.Bennett.
  Turnstone Press 1978.
  A profound study of the situation of man in the world and the
  way in which energy transformations are involved in religious
  work.

Energies by J.G.Bennett.
Coombe Springs Press 1964.
An outline of a unique theory of energy relatedness and the way that energies may be used alchemically for personal development.

The Alchemists by F.Sherwood Taylor.
Heineman 1952.
A very useful introduction to the subject of Alchemy as the precursor of Chemistry.

The Alchemical Writings of Edward Kelly translated by A.E.Waite.
Vincent Stuart and J.M.Watkins 1980.
A typical set of Alchemical treatises written in the usual enigmatic style, though with a certain charm, by a man who cheated many of the crowned heads of Europe before his execution.

Alchemy the secret art by S.K. de Rola.
Avon Books and Thames and Hudson London.
A basic introduction to philosophical Alchemy, particularly useful for the many, beautiful reproductions of pictures and illustrations taken from some very rare Alchemical texts.

The Theory of Celestial Influence by Rodney Collin.
Robinson and Watkins 1980.
An outstanding book on a modern theory of Astrology, quite unlike any of the more traditional texts and based on the system of Gurdjieff and Ouspensky.

SECTION 4.

Hamlet's Mill by G. de Santillana and H. von Dechend.
Gambit Inc.(Boston) 1969.
A difficult though remarkable essay on the Astronomical basis of myth.

A Kabbalistic Universe by Z'ev ben Shimon Halevi.
Gateway Books, Bath.
A remarkably frank exposition on the hitherto hidden teachings of Jewish Kabbalah in relation to traditional cosmology by a leading contemporary teacher.

City of Revelation by John Michell.
Abacus/Sphere 1973
The application of gematria to the study of architecture and its relationship with the cosmic model of the temple.

Occidental Mythology by Joseph Campbell.
Souvenir Press 1964.
One in a series called 'The Masks of God'. This volume deals with the mythology and symbolism of the west including Mithraism.

Heresy by Joan O'Grady
Element Books 1985
A good book for finding out what were the major heresies of the early church and how they arose.

Index